MY TORTURED CONSCIENCE

Martin Weber

REVIEW AND HERALD® PUBLISHING ASSOCIATION
WASHINGTON, DC 20039-0555
HAGERSTOWN, MD 21740

This book was
Edited by Richard W. Coffen
Designed by Bill Kirstein
Cover photo by Dennis Crews
Typeset: 11/12 Korinna

PRINTED IN U.S.A.

96 95 94 93 92 91   10 9 8 7 6 5 4 3 2 1

Library of Congress Cataloging-in-Publication Data

Weber, Martin, 1951–
  My tortured conscience / Martin Weber.
      p.   cm.
    1. Weber, Martin, 1951– . 2. Seventh-day Adventists—United States
—Clergy—Biography. 3. Adventists—United States—Clergy—Biography.
4. Sabbatarians—United   States—Clergy—Biography.   5. Justification.
6. Conscience—Religious aspects—Seventh-day Adventists. 7. Seventh-
day Adventists—Doctrines. I. Title. BX6193.W42A3 1991
286.7'092—dc20
[B]   90-47056
                                                              CIP

ISBN 0-8280-0605-9

Contents

Preface

I used to rob banks, smuggle dope, and drink until dawn. Then I met Jesus, and He changed my life completely!" So goes the typical testimony heard on Christian talk shows. We love these stories of prodigals who went over the cliff into sin's follies before coming home to their heavenly Father.

My story is different. I went over fool's hill in the opposite extreme, plunging into the depths of legalism. My hyperactive conscience, yearning to please God, robbed me of friends, family, scholarships, health, and nearly life itself. God's mercy saved me just in time.

Frankly, much of what you will read in these pages is information I'd rather you didn't know—it's embarrassing. For nine years I never told my story publicly. Then several years ago, a spiritual leader whom I admire invited me to share my testimony of a tortured conscience with a group of his friends. He thought the story of my struggles would encourage many, and so it did. I fervently wish the same for you.

In these pages I mention several people who brought pain into my life. Please understand that I'm not criticizing any of them. Everyone meant well—from my parents to pastors, teachers, and other Christian friends who have offered spiritual guidance. I appreciate their sincere efforts—and pray that the peace of God which now reigns in my heart will find a home in theirs as well.

I write with special gratitude to my mother. God never gave anyone a more dedicated, delightful mom than I have. Deepest thanks also to Steve Gifford, Tom Mostert, J. Wayne Coulter, and Herman Bauman, all of them Seventh-day Adventist Church leaders who have brightened my life more than they can know.

Named After a Jewish Hero

1

BEAUTIFUL FRÄULEIN!" snarled the hulking soldier as he staggered toward the slender young widow, intending to attack her. World War II was over in the castle village of Heidenheim, Germany. But this officer of the American occupation army had vowed his own revenge upon the defeated foe. Stalking the streets for a victim one afternoon, he spotted Hildegard Anke sitting alone in her yard, sewing in the sunshine.

The drunken major approached the startled woman, demanding, "Who killed my father?"

Hildegard sat terror-struck as the huge man with a blond crew cut pulled out a knife from his belt. Had God brought her safely through the war only to let her die in her own yard on this peaceful afternoon?

"You'd better tell me who killed them!" he bellowed.

Just then two other American soldiers appeared. Sneaking up behind the officer, they motioned for Hildegard to keep quiet.

"Tell me who did it!" the man shrieked, brandishing his knife.

Finally Hildegard whispered, "It must have been the Germans."

"You're—right!" he yelled. "You Germans killed my father, my brother, and my friends. So now I'm going to kill you."

He edged closer while the other two Americans crept up behind him. "Beautiful Fräulein!" he growled softly through an evil smirk. Then, gesturing with a slit across his throat, he added: "Beautiful red blood!"

Knife flashing in the sunlight, with a sudden rabid roar, he lunged toward Hildegard. He grabbed her shoulder, ripping her dress as she tried to flee. Just before the knife plunged into her neck, the other two Americans got him in a bear hug and wrestled him out of the yard. They pushed him down the street toward their medic van and got him sobered up.

One of those two heroes was Martin Wolf Cohen. He was a Jew, yet he risked his life to save a German. I am proud to be named after him.

That stabbing attempt wasn't the only close call my mother suffered during Hitler's awful war. One time the murderer of millions himself unwittingly saved her life. She was riding the afternoon train to Nuremberg when, for no apparent reason, they were sidetracked. For more than an hour the passengers waited, wondering what the delay might be. Suddenly the *Sonderzug,* Hitler's private train, sped past, racing north toward Berlin. Before my mother's train could recover from the delay and proceed south, hell broke loose on the horizon.

Allied planes were bombing Nuremburg, turning the railroad station into an inferno. Were it not for the delay caused by Hitler's train, my mother would have been sitting in the station to wait for her connection. Everyone in the waiting room perished.

Time after time my mother survived life-threatening situations. Her husband Walter didn't. He met his death in Operation Barbarossa, Hitler's mad invasion of the Soviet Union.

With her beloved buried in an unmarked grave outside Kiev, my mother fled to Munich to find comfort with her older brother Herbert. He had been a Luftwaffe pilot early in the war, flying reconnaissance missions over England. A shrapnel wound that collapsed his lungs forced an early discharge from military duty.

Soon after my mother arrived in Munich, that city also suffered the Allies' just revenge. Night after night our bombers screamed overhead, dropping their thunderous retribution. Fearing for his sister's life, Herbert sent her away to the rural area of south-central Germany to find refuge with their aunt.

A medieval castle overlooks the picturesque village of Heidenheim. Hitler turned the castle into barracks for his notorious SS soldiers, who commandeered the local citizenry. My mother found herself designated an air-raid warden. As such she had to attend weekly Sunday morning briefings, held at the same time as services at St. Paul's Lutheran Church. She decided to risk the wrath of the SS by skipping their meetings for the sake of weekly worship. Not that she was particularly religious at the time, but as a grieving widow she drew strength from church fellowship.

One day she found an official notice posted on her door. Its message was crisp and to the point: "Be warned that if you are not present at our meeting Sunday morning, you will face dire consequences."

The SS meant business. Next Sunday afternoon heavy footsteps pounded up the stairs toward her apartment. Two SS soldiers burst inside and found her in the bedroom. "We warned you not to miss our meeting. Now you pay the price."

They tossed two burlap sacks at her and ordered, "Get out of bed and put your things in these bags. Then come with us."

"But I'm sick with the flu. I can't get out of bed."

"That's too bad," they scoffed. "We'll be glad to help you pack." With that they stuffed some of her clothes into the sacks and hustled her outside to their truck. As she shivered with fever in the chill November air, they tied a black blindfold around her eyes and raced out of town. Mile after mile they bounced down country roads. Finally they squealed to a stop in the middle of nowhere.

"Here we are," announced the soldiers, removing the blindfold.

"Take a look at your new home. You won't have to worry about missing any meetings out here."

Before her lay a bombed-out farmhouse without even a roof. Just a few walls surrounded by nail-strewn ashes. "We hope you'll be comfortable here," the SS men jeered as they jumped into their truck and roared off. For a few minutes my mother watched the cloud of dust following them down the road. Then she crept toward the ruins and collapsed on top of them. Where else was there to go?

That night as she shivered under the stars, Allied bombers roared overhead. She felt an unlikely consolation watching the dark forms streak across the moon—at least she wasn't alone in her exile. But was this all there was left to her life? "Lord," she cried, "let one of the bombs fall on me. I can't take it anymore." Not long afterward she mercifully passed out. When she woke up, she found herself in the Heidenheim Hospital. How she got there she has no idea.

Finally the terrors of the war were past, and the ravaged world began to heal. For young widows, as well, life would go on. That meant meeting new men. A new friend appeared on the scene to light up my mother's life—Karl Benz, a relative of the automobile makers. They fell in love.

One evening they were out dancing in the upstairs ballroom of the concert hall. An American soldier followed them inside. Tall, dark-haired Fred Weber had been scouting Hildegard for several days, and he liked what he saw. He was not about to let Karl Benz have such a prize as Hildegard.

He decided to dispense with his rival. Confronting the dancing couple, he ushered Karl to the door and shoved him down the stairs. Mr. Benz crawled onto his motorcycle and rode off, never to return.

With my father's rival out of the way, it was time to turn on the charm. He already knew where my mother lived, and the next morning she found a Christmas tree at her doorstep—a rare treat in war-torn Germany. That was only the beginning. My father spared nothing to win her favor. When he learned how much she liked cats, he got himself a cat at the snack bar that he managed for the army. Not one cat, or two, or five, but thirteen cats! He even climbed a mountain and brought back the legendary Edelweiss, the flower for lovers.

Naturally my mother was charmed by this amazing American—yet she was homesick to be reunited with her brother at their childhood home in Saxony. It was no simple matter to go back east into the Russian zone, but after weeks of waiting, the permission papers finally arrived.

"Let me see those papers," my father asked pleasantly. He took them from her hand and stalked over to the wood stove. One brief flare of the flames, and my mother's hopes became ashes.

"What are you doing!" she screamed.

"Forget those silly papers," he smiled. "I'll get you some better papers that will bring you to America."

Right about this time my mother had to be hospitalized. The chief of staff warned her, "After you get better, don't even consider going with that soldier to America."

But day by day as her charming suitor came in with flowers for her and candy for the hospital staff, everybody began to like him. One day a nurse remarked, "The only kind of flowers he hasn't brought you yet are tea roses." You guessed it—the next day in came a huge vase of tea roses! Shaking his head in disbelief, the head doctor declared, "With that man I will let you go to Siberia."

My mother's uncle Erich wasn't quite so sure about him. He had a lot of experience evaluating men, having been a captain in the German Army. When he felt strongly about someone, he didn't mind letting his opinion be known. In fact, he may have been the only man in the military who called Hitler's general field marshal Rommel a pig—and lived to laugh about it.

His encounter with the famed and feared Desert Fox happened during one of Hitler's military campaigns. Uncle Erich saw a fellow officer shamelessly urinating in the freshly fallen snow. He groused, "What kind of swine would do a thing like that!"

The officer whirled around. It was Rommel himself! Seeing Erich's astonished face, he grinned. "You're right. I guess I am a swine."

Uncle Erich had a habit of speaking up for principle. One time near the end of the war it nearly cost him his life. Himmler, czar of the concentration camps, gave orders to evacuate Dachau. Wanting to clear the camp of prisoners before the advancing American army could liberate them, he loaded them into railroad cars and sent them south toward Austria.

Meanwhile, Uncle Erich was marching his men north toward Munich to fight the Americans. Suddenly they came upon this train that had stopped, with Jewish prisoners milling around the tracks. Uncle Erich was shocked at their emaciated appearance—and even more aghast at the order of the SS commander: "Have your men help us line up these prisoners so we can shoot them."

"Shoot innocent civilians?"

"They're just Jewish scum. Useless eaters. We've got orders to get rid of them before the Americans get here. You'd better cooperate."

11

"No! My men will not participate. The Wehrmacht are soldiers, not murderers."

"Do you realize the consequences of disobeying an order of the Führer's SS?"

Uncle Erich's conscience did allow him to participate in Hitler's unjust adventurism, but he refused to massacre innocent civilians. Furious, the SS commander sentenced him to be shot. Before the execution could take place, the roar of approaching American tanks forced the Germans to deal with other business at hand. Uncle Erich's act of heroism on behalf of Jewish prisoners was not forgotten. After the war he received a special citation from the Allied de-Nazification council in Stuttgart.

Having returned from combat to his home in Heidenheim, he wasn't sure what to think about this young American sergeant courting his favorite niece. Little things about Fred Weber bothered him. Like how he kept tracking mud into the house even after they specially provided slippers for him. Uncle Erich warned my mother, "Since your father died, I've felt responsible for you. Listen to me—if you leave us now to marry this man, you will regret it."

She thought her uncle was just prejudiced against an enemy soldier, unable to see the good in his character. So she ignored his advice and married Fred Weber. Soon the couple announced they were moving to America. Before they left, little Freddie was born. At 10 weeks of age he was the youngest baby up to that point to fly across the ocean with Pan Am. The flight attendants had their picture taken with him en route to New York's La Guardia Airport.

The little Weber family settled in the northern New Jersey suburb of Clifton. One evening they returned from their swimming club to find a white card stuck in the door of their brick apartment building. My father reached for it and looked it over. It was an enrollment card for the free Bible correspondence course of the Faith for Today telecast. He handed it to my mother. "Looks like a good opportunity for you to learn to read English."

"But they won't understand my German scribbling."

"Oh, I'm sure they have people who can translate."

So my mother became a student of the Seventh-day Adventist message. Back and forth the lessons went. Then one day there was a knock on the door. Two smiling men stood on the porch—Elder Hayes from the nearby Adventist church with one of the local elders.

"Come in," my mother welcomed. Somehow one of her long, dangling earrings fell on the floor, and the pastor accidentally crunched it under his shoe.

"Don't worry," my mother consoled the embarrassed man. "Here, we're just sitting down to dinner. Come join us."

The pastor spotted pork chops on the table and politely declined.

"Well, at least have a glass of wine with us," my mother insisted. "It's our favorite kind, Virginia Dare."

No thanks again. It wasn't exactly a storybook soul-winning visit. Nevertheless, the pastor made friends with the family and invited them to church. "We have lots of German members, Hildegard. You would certainly enjoy the ladies' Tuesday morning Dorcas meetings."

She did. The fellowship won her heart. Although some of the Dorcas ladies were a bit overanxious to take off Mother's jewelry, she liked them all just the same. Even so, she wasn't quite ready to be baptized.

About that time I was getting ready to be born. It was my mother's second cesarean operation, and there were complications. Doctors could administer only local anesthesia. As the pain increased and the medication had to be strengthened, my mother felt a numbness creep over her heart. The doctors feared they might be losing her.

"Lord, please don't let me die," she pleaded. "What would happen to my two babies? If You let me live with this baby, I promise to be baptized."

One last bit of drama occurred before we left the hospital. When the nurses brought the babies to the mothers for feeding, they put the wrong boy in her arms.

"He's not my Marty," she protested.

"Sure he is," the nurses insisted. A vigorous discussion ensued. Finally a half hour later they found the real me.

Well, my mother kept her promise and was baptized into the

Adventist Church. My father did not object. In fact, he had an interest in getting baptized himself—although he didn't care for all our doctrines. For one thing, there was no way he was going to surrender his life to be controlled by the writings of Ellen G. White. He had other questions as well that kept him from joining any church group, although the late Herbert Armstrong's Worldwide Church of God strongly influenced his beliefs. Since Armstrong's group doesn't welcome visitors who like to argue, my father has always attended Adventist churches.

It wasn't easy for my mother to forsake her Lutheran heritage. Not only did she grow up in Saxony, homeland of Luther, but her ancestors had been Lutherans going back to the 1500s. Because of such deep roots, I always assumed that I was named after Martin Luther. Then in the past couple years I learned about Martin Wolf Cohen, the Jewish man who saved my mother's life.

I found myself more than a little curious about meeting him. Could I possibly sweep back 40 years of dust and find the man for whom I am named? I had to try. My mother told me which part of America he had come from. She also recalled that his family owned a store. Armed with that information, I found myself in that area earlier this year. With a couple hours to spare, I went to a phone booth and looked up the name Cohen. There were some listings for "M. Cohen" and even one or two for "Martin Cohen." Excitedly I dialed the numbers. Nothing doing. Nobody I talked with had been a soldier in World War II, nor did they know anyone of that name who had.

There was just one number left. I called it several times, but nobody ever answered. Finally I gave up. When I returned home, I slipped the phone number into my file and forgot about it. Until today. While looking for my mortgage payment booklet, I came across the little yellow scrap of paper with Martin Cohen's number on it.

Wouldn't hurt to call again, I thought. After several rings a lady answered.

"Is this the home of Martin Wolf Cohen?" I asked eagerly.

"Yes, how may I help you?"

"I'm Martin Weber calling from the West Coast, and I'd like to speak with him, please."

"I'm on the line," he answered from another extension.

"Mr. Cohen, were you an American soldier in Germany during World War II—stationed afterward in the castle village of Heidenheim?"

"Why, yes," he answered, hesitantly. "I was in the medic armor division there. What about it?"

"You've never met me, but I'm named after you. That's because you saved my mother's life!"

"But I don't remember saving anybody's life. What's your mother's name?"

"Hildegard. She was the widow of Walter Anke."

"I remember a Hilde over there, but I don't remember saving her life."

"Well, would you tell me what you look like?"

"I'm about five feet seven inches, with dark eyes. Back then I had wavy black hair."

It was the exact description my mother gave me of him. She had also mentioned that they were the same age.

"Mind if I ask your age?" I ventured.

"I just turned 68."

"So did my mother!"

"I guess I must be the one she told you about—but I just don't remember saving her life."

"Well," I suggested, "maybe it happened on a day when there was lots of other action. That's probably why you don't recall it. One thing is certain. There aren't too many five-foot-seven-inch 68-year-old Jewish men in your city named Martin Wolf Cohen who were medic soldiers in the German village of Heidenheim and remember knowing Hildegard."

What a conversation. Mrs. Cohen invited me to visit them the next time I'm in their part of the country. I'm looking forward to it.

Recently I had the opportunity to fly overseas with my mother and visit Heidenheim. Together we explored its streets and shops. So much had changed since the war, yet much remains the same. The castle is still there, majestically guarding the village in the valley. So is St. Paul's Lutheran Church, where my parents were married. My mother and I looked inside the concert hall where she met my father, and we ordered hot chocolate in the same coffee shop where they once sat and talked. We even went to the home where Martin Wolf Cohen saved her life—and an elderly neighbor who witnessed the scene told me all about it.

All this is of great interest to me as I approach my fortieth birthday. With senility lurking around the corner, I find myself reminiscing a lot, probing my roots to discover what made my parents what they are so I can understand myself better. It's important for each of us to know how the Lord has been leading in our past so we can trust Him for the future. Don't you think?

I wrote this life story of mine, which you are reading, for the sake of your relationship with God. You see, in my quest for peace of mind, I've fought a vicious war. Not in Germany or Vietnam, but a war in my heart coping with a tyrant more deadly than Hitler—the tyrant of a guilty conscience. Christ has helped me win that battle, and He can lift the burden for you, too.

See what you think as you read these pages.

Burned Out on Religion

2

BE STILL, and know that I am God." This solemn warning in Gothic gold letters adorned the church sanctuary I attended as a child in the North Jersey suburbs of New York City.

" 'Be still' means sit still!" my kindergarten Bible class teachers admonished. Seeking to instill us with reverence, they warned that God got upset when children twisted around in church. One of them testified, "Even if a firecracker exploded behind me in church, I wouldn't turn around." It seemed that God got mad if my head itched and I scratched it while worshiping Him.

Church school teachers said that the Lord could take to heaven only perfect children (who obviously didn't itch much and always tied their shoes). The rest of us He loved very much, but too bad. . . . Then our teachers added brightly, "Jesus promises to take away your naughty hearts and give you clean hearts—if you ask Him and really, really mean it."

Well, I bowed my head then and there, asking God to please give me that clean heart. But He didn't do it. My young conscience wagged its bony finger in my face and damned me to hell.

Sure, God loves me, my childish mind reasoned, *but He also loved mean old Hitler. Both of us will burn together.* So it was that fear of Christ's disfavor froze the buds of first faith.

Without question, my childhood spiritual guardians did their honest best. "Fear God and keep His commandments," they cautioned. "Every time you yell at your brother, an angel makes a black mark in the books of heaven. And If you die with a black mark on your record, you'll be lost. So when you run around the playground, and all through the day, whisper a prayer that God will forgive your sins. And when you kneel down at night, make sure all your marks of sin are erased before you go to sleep."

At home, my father modeled his parenting after the military. He loved the Army, having won the Silver Star back in Germany for risking his life to defuse a mine field. He determined to turn our house into something of a boot camp.

My father's discipline left no time for foolishness. He announced that he would put our TV on the curb with a dollar bill taped to the top for anyone who would take it away. So out went Howdy Doody and Captain Kangaroo, replaced by big red encyclopedia sets and colorful Bible story books. Our neighbors were astounded that children not old enough to attend kindergarten could read the front page of the Bergen *Evening Record*. We memorized daily Bible verses, too.

I'm glad my father had strict standards for my two brothers and me to live up to. What we could have done without is the atmosphere of ridicule and intimidation, especially in a religious setting. We imagined God to be the stern commander in chief of the universe, forever fuming about childish shortcomings.

Morning by morning the big white clock radio crackled awake at 5:45, in plenty of time for daily family worship. My father lined us up on the threadbare couch to read from his big, black hardcover Bible. Deuteronomy 28 was his favorite chapter, the last half of it pronouncing curse after curse from the Almighty upon rebellious sinners. We all knelt on the black tile floor and had to pray forever. Sometimes for 20 minutes.

Afternoons when we got home from school, a long list of duties awaited us. My father would often appear unannounced to check up on his sons' obedience. Fred, the oldest, was always doing exactly as ordered. Often my younger brother, Bill, and I had sneaked outside to play, keeping our ears alert. The sound of squealing brakes was our signal. Daddy's coming! We had about four and a half seconds to scramble inside the house before his big red plumbing truck rounded the corner.

To this day my father proudly proclaims his gospel of fear and force. Although my brothers and I were A students, we failed emotionally. At least I did. Throughout life I've been afraid of anyone who wields authority—pastors, school principals, and employers. I can testify that scholastic excellence isn't worth much without personal confidence and self-worth. Given the choice, I'll take security over brilliance any day. Only during the past 10 years have I been feeling good about myself. (I'll explain later.)

Even a dark sky has its stars. The star of my life is my mother. People tell me they have never met a more loving, delightful person. Mom did her best to shelter us from my father's excesses. "Let them go to sleep now," she pleaded in her German accent, trying to bring to a merciful end some marathon Bible study session.

"You stay out of this!" he ordered.

Mom seldom prevailed with her intercessions, although she kept trying. The problem was that my father assumed absolute authority and forbade her soothing influence from interfering with the fear of Yahweh.

Sometimes Mom ran away with us. We would hurry to the corner and catch the first bus going in either direction—only to return a week or so later when our few dollars ran out.

Church members knew about the problems in our home. Their expressions of comfort and support meant much. Unfortunately, the legalism they struggled with prevented them from lifting our spiritual burden.

When I was about 10, a long white envelope arrived from the new pastor's wife. Mom opened it excitedly—how nice to get a personal letter from the parsonage! It was about me. Mom's smile faded as she read: "Dear Sister Weber, some of us in the prayer group have noticed that Marty has become quite chubby. We fear for his salvation. If your son ever hopes to make it to heaven, he's just got to lose some weight."

Bless her heart. The good woman felt alarmed for me, so she sent some threats from the throne of grace to help me get to heaven. She even included several yellow sheets on which she had typed a diet of natural foods. It listed things like sesame seeds, sunflower seeds, millet, and so forth. At first I got mad. Then I scoffed, "This stuff is what they make into Hartz Mountain bird food! It's for the birds!"

In retrospect, parakeets and canaries are quite healthy as they chirp happily, hopping around their cages. My diet now isn't much different from what the pastor's wife recommended. (I do indulge in frozen yogurt whenever I get my hands on a discount coupon, and every Friday night our family enjoys homemade chocolate chip cookies and Nestle's Crunch ice-cream bars.)

All things considered, I think that pastor's wife would be pleased with me now. As a chubby child, however, I didn't need my salvation threatened any more than it already was. Besides, all I needed to forfeit my baby fat was an adolescent growth spurt.

Keep in mind, though, the pastor's wife meant well. It took real courage to mail my mother that epistle of doom for chubby Marty. If only she would have included some expression of warmth or confidence, like: "I've noticed Marty always marks his little green Bible during the sermon." But no. She herself seemed imprisoned in a spiritual Siberia, devoid of hope or joy. How could she pass along to me what she lacked herself?

Meanwhile, at home things kept getting worse. Finally, when I was 12, Mom scraped together $100 from mending clothes so we could escape for good. We managed to rent a tiny apartment in a rundown neighborhood.

Friends from the local Baptist and Catholic churches surprised us with bags of groceries. Several members of my mother's Adventist church showed concern as well. From her own funds, the principal of our church school paid full tuition for my brothers and me. Our new pastor, noticing holes in my shoes, took me to Garden State Plaza and bought me the shiniest pair of black loafers I had ever owned. No question about it, he was a deeply committed Christian.

Our family lived in constant fear that my father would discover our hideout. He did. One day when Mom wasn't home, he suddenly ducked inside our doorway. The cat ran under the bed, Fred jumped out the window, and Bill and I scattered elsewhere.

Mom didn't want to divorce my father, and she hasn't to this day. Only the Lord knows the hardship she has endured. Since her German office skills meant nothing in America, the only work she could find at first was a clerk's job at Eastern Freightways, a trucking company, which paid her only the minimum wage. Many nights she washed windows and scrubbed floors so she could make the payments on our rusted Chevy lowrider. I cooked for my brothers and went to the

Laundromat. Our thrift-store clothes weren't fancy, but they were comfortable—except for the long-remembered day I accidentally starched my brothers' underwear. Poor Bill and Fred scratched and itched like crazy. (Good thing they weren't in church at the time!)

The summer of 1964 our pastor visited us every week to prepare my brothers and me for baptism. I came up from the water dripping with happiness, feeling wonderfully close to God. But my joy didn't last long. You see, a dear old lady asked us for a ride home—then she got to talking with her friends. For a half hour she kept us waiting in the car.

I felt myself getting angry. Immediately, a sinking feeling struck me—I still didn't have that new heart after all! By the time we pulled up to our apartment, I was slouched in the back seat, condemning myself as a hypocrite. What good had it done to get baptized? I was still a lost soul.

Well, life went on. Every spring and fall the pastor or some visiting preacher came by our school to conduct a Week of Spiritual Emphasis. Arching their eyebrows, they exclaimed: "Jesus has all the strength you need to live above sin so that you can be safe for God to take to heaven. Mercy lingers, but soon the door of probation will close. We who have great light but don't live up to it are grieving away the Holy Spirit. Even now, some of you may be committing the unpardonable sin by resisting the power of the Spirit to change your life."

Several of my classmates wondered whether they had already committed this dreadful sin. "What's the use even trying?" they lamented. So they exchanged their Bibles for transistor radios. Rock music was much easier to understand than religion, and a lot more fun.

Our teachers and the pastor became alarmed at the growing popularity of the Beatles and the Beach Boys. During Week of Prayer time, the visiting speaker gave an especially fervent appeal to follow God. The kids squirmed in embarrassed silence, hoping the ordeal wouldn't last too long. While the organ played "Just as I Am," the speaker dabbed at his eyes with his neatly ironed handkerchief. I clenched my fists and strode up the aisle, determined to show God and my classmates that I wasn't ashamed of taking a stand.

Back home that night, kneeling in the darkness of my room, I begged God, "Please, oh, please give me Your free gift of a new heart so I won't want to sin anymore!" At last I drifted off to sleep, really believing that this time the Lord had heard my prayer. Next morning, though, I woke up late. The sun was already shining, and I'd be tardy for school. To make matters worse, my brother was taking too long in the bathroom. I got upset. So much for my new heart.

Well, I had lost another round with religion. When would I ever become like Jesus so I could be saved?

One hot summer day after eighth-grade graduation I was alone in our upstairs apartment while I played a record on our phonograph. Listening to those beautiful songs about heaven, my heart sank with the realization that I would never make it there. I collapsed facedown on the couch and sobbed, "Oh God, how much I want that new heart! Why won't You give it to me?"

Social Insecurity

3

THE YEAR 1969 left the world with many memories. People first set foot on the moon, an unforgettable scientific achievement. That summer also brought us Woodstock, an unrivaled entertainment festival. In October came the Vietnam War Moratorium in Washington, an unprecedented protest rally.

In my personal life as well, the year 1969 was memorable. It brought me unforgettable failure, unrivaled sadness, and unprecedented isolation. I was a senior attending Garden State Academy, a Christian boarding school in the New Jersey town of Tranquility. Yet life for me was anything but tranquil there.

My inner turmoil swirled around a lack of self-esteem. For one thing, I felt socially inferior to my classmates. This had its roots in childhood, when my father didn't let me go roller skating on Saturday nights. "It's worldly and a waste of time," he declared, making me practice the piano instead. Being baby-sat by Beethoven isn't as much fun as going to a party, let me assure you. By the time the family separated when I was 12, my inferiority complex had me in a stranglehold that endured for many years.

The girls at Garden State Academy didn't bolster my sense of self-worth. It seemed they had formed a cartel of sorts to determine which of them would date what boy. I don't know if they had a secret lottery or what. Of course, the popular fellows just went ahead and dated whomever they wished, but the rest of us were stuck with the system. The girl selected for me was sweet, but she didn't turn me on. The girls I wanted lived on the moon, as far as their availability to me. I became convinced that nobody halfway desirable would ever want to marry me. Quite a depressing thought.

One of the big social disasters for me that school year was Pioneer Day, commemorating nineteenth-century church founders. The girls sewed themselves long dresses and bonnets, and the guys sprouted sideburns and beards. I didn't even have respectable peach fuzz yet, in painful contrast to some of my peers who flaunted their physical maturity.

I was always the youngest in my class from first grade on up, a discomforting situation now compounded by belated adolescence. Hopeless uncoordination mocked my love for sports. My spectacular catches of simple fly balls became legendary. I fantasized about home runs but never hit a ball even near the fence. In basketball I pictured myself doing slam dunks, yet I couldn't even shoot free throws reliably. Magic Johnson I wasn't. I even made a semi-fool of myself playing ping-pong.

Nevertheless, I was a nice guy and so had friends, several of them remarkably loyal. But for the most part it was "Hey, wait for me!" You can understand why I never ran for class office. No way. My peers wouldn't have voted for me to be the campus dogcatcher.

You think I'm exaggerating? Only a little bit. The faculty sponsor did acknowledge my scholastic endeavors by arranging the assignment of Student Association representative. Just the right job for a nerd who deserved a bit of recognition. Membership in the in crowd continued to elude me.

Desperate for attention, I made a pest out of myself by reciting stupid knock-knock jokes. The girls would snort in disgust, "Why don't you grow up!" Some of the faculty likewise disdained my presence.

Social insecurity. Turmoil in Tranquility.

Why am I sharing this embarrassing stuff about my past? Well, if you have ever struggled with self-esteem, maybe what I'm going to say can help you. I'm not proud of myself, that's for sure—but I am proud of the Lord. You see, I just attended my twentieth high school class reunion, and my old classmates couldn't hide their astonishment about what has happened in my life. The truth is that many of them didn't even recognize me. You'll understand why as you keep reading these pages.

Back in high school I took revenge for social insecurity by trying to clobber fellow classmates academically. If I couldn't make the grade at Saturday night's social, I certainly could pour on the points during Monday morning's physics test.

Brandishing brainpower did nothing to enhance my popularity. Regardless of that, I determined to become class valedictorian, thus proving my worth to my peers so I could exit in glory on graduation day. Even here I failed, however, falling short of my goal by a couple hundredths of a point. That's all there was separating me from number one. A miserable fraction of a point—just enough to perpetuate the curse that befogged my life.

That May afternoon when the valedictory award was announced, in bitter tears I rode my bicycle home. I could hardly see the road in my thunderstorm of grief. "Why, God?" I wailed as I pedaled along. I ranted against the school principal, accusing him of manipulating the grading system to favor my rival, undoubtedly a pet of his. Ultimately, however, I could blame only myself, and so I pounded the handlebars in frustration. "Can't I make good in anything? Anything at all!"

Looking back now, I realize I had nothing to be ashamed of academically. Nor did the worthy valedictorian, who became my college roommate and whose friendship endures to this day. Both of us won scholarships. Nevertheless, I regret that academic dogfight.

So I failed in my great goal of becoming valedictorian. Though depressed about that, I had no time to wallow in self-pity. Every dime of my tuition had to be paid before graduation. Nobody was writing checks on my behalf, so every afternoon it was off to the furniture factory to stain redwood benches.

The manager there didn't seem to like me any more than the academy principal did. Much of that was my own fault—I have to admit I wasn't all that lovable. When a boy lacks a fulfilling relationship with his father, he usually has difficulty relating to others, especially those who wield power over him.

Not that I was rebellious, you understand. I worked and studied hard, never breaking any rules. I craved the goodwill of my leaders and teachers, but was scared of them and skeptical of their motives. Many of them sensed my alienation and bounced it back at me. Others were nothing but decent.

My sole refuge from the turmoil in Tranquility was Mr. Manley, a dear old Black man who was my supervisor at the furniture factory. He didn't make much money, but he made a lot of people happy. Above the roar of the yellow forklift trucks you could hear him howling with laughter—a sure sign he had just told one of his amazing jokes.

His favorite was about two Black men in Mississippi who were walking alongside the road minding their own business when a White man in a pickup truck purposely steered into them. One of the victims crashed through the windshield and the other flew off into a cotton field. When the sheriff came along, he decided to file charges. He charged the first Black man with breaking and entering—and the second one with leaving the scene of an accident.

Mr. Manley had suffered prejudice aplenty during his six decades, and he survived by laughing off the ignorance of racism and by nurturing a faith in God that yielded solid self-respect. Occasionally he got discouraged and disgusted by the rampant hypocrisy, but nothing could make him stop loving everyone. At breaktime he would go over to the 7-Up machine, drop in some coins, and bring back frosty green bottles. Sometimes he also bought pizza for the student workers.

Old Mr. Manley took a personal interest in me. The only fatherly advice I got as a teenager came from him. He wasn't a theologian, yet he knew more about life than most seminary graduates. Most important, I knew he was praying for me—I needed all the prayer I could get. You see, even worse than my social insecurity was my spiritual confusion.

Memorizing millions of inspired quotations in Bible class didn't help. Those carefully chosen passages enjoined upon our teenage consciences the burden of attaining absolute perfection of character. Only thus could we be saved by Christ, the teacher assured us. Sadly, the end result of all that memorization was not salvation but discouragement and spiritual paralysis.

One pleasant religious experience came every Friday night after vespers. We would "walk and talk with God" around the lake. I felt close to my Creator and, with crickets chirping in the background, reverently recommitted my life to Him. But then the next morning I woke up as usual. Nothing had changed—I was still the same stupid sinner.

This wretched perplexity I had already suffered as a child, you recall—expecting God to bless spiritual commitment by giving me a holy heart. I thought that any truly born-again teenager would surely lose his appetite for such indulgences as sex before marriage and even ice cream. He would enjoy spending Sunday afternoons at the local nursing home watching the old ladies knit and reading them the book of Deuteronomy. So I imagined.

Not until years later did I learn the truth about the new heart experience. Being reborn in Christ doesn't mean spiritual goose bumps will bristle all day long. It won't make us feel like praying before dawn when the alarm shatters our sleep. Actually, many cravings for sin remain with us throughout life, clinging to us like summer fleas on a cat.

Don't take my word for it. Here's how the Bible describes every Christian's struggle: "The flesh [sinful human nature] sets its desire against the Spirit, and the Spirit against the flesh; for these are in opposition to one another, so that *you may not do the things that you please*" (Gal. 5:17, NASB).

You get the picture? The flesh whispers, "If it feels good, do it!" while the Spirit warns, "Only if God says so." Despite deep commitment to obey God's voice in our conscience, sinful human nature lingers to harass us. Even after we pray, "Lead us not into temptation," temptation yet abounds—not just from the world outside but from within ourselves: "Each one is tempted when he is drawn away by his own desires and enticed" (James 1:14, NKJV). The apostle acknowledges inner enticement. No doubt this included the temptation to eat too much, lose one's temper, and fantasize about forbidden sex. And this despite the new heart experience.

While there is much we can do to distance ourselves from temptation, we can't escape the cravings within. Does this mean we must yield to sin? Definitely not! Any true believer yearns to honor God and stop fooling around with sin. We don't want to hurt ourselves or other people by indulging in disordered behavior. Well, then, why doesn't God just take those cravings away?

Good question. Let's think about it. What would happen if God removed all temptation to be impatient, to overeat, to lust, to be greedy? Without sinful flesh we might forget our need to trust in Christ for our salvation! We would become religious peacocks, like the Pharisee in the Temple who strutted his self-righteousness. "God, I thank Thee that I'm not like that sinner over there." Temptation keeps us humble with the continual reminder that "in me (that is, in my flesh) nothing good dwells" (Rom. 7:18, NKJV).

Furthermore, suffering our own sinful cravings reminds us why our neighbors enjoy visiting Las Vegas. It's much easier reaching their hearts when we can relate to their spiritual needs because of our own struggles. What's more, resisting temptation continually reaffirms our commitment to live for Christ.

Understanding all this, we see that suffering those awful enticements isn't such a bad idea. So why agonize about all the evil vampires in the dark corners of our minds? Don't chase them around, vainly trying to capture them. Leave them alone —God doesn't hold us accountable for the sinful lusts we were born with! Turn your attention to Jesus, thanking God for His mercy and His power.

All right, you may be thinking. *But what about that man who stood up in church and testified: "For 40 years I smoked more cigarettes than the Marlboro Man. Then God gave me a new heart, and now I don't even* want *to light up!"* As the congregation murmured fervent amens, you sat there feeling guilty because you still struggle with cravings for fooling around with sin.

Well, what about it? Does God remove some temptations but not others? Let's consider this carefully. What did that man really mean in his testimony? Was he saying "I don't *feel* like sinning anymore—I've got holy flesh"? Or rather "I don't want to live like a fool again by yielding to those terrible lusts that continue to haunt me"? Do you see the difference?

Something else to notice is that temptations come in different types. Some would abuse the natural functions of the body, such as food and sex. Others involve artificial activities like smoking (we don't have smokestacks emerging from our heads), narcotics (our noses weren't designed to snort cocaine), gambling (we weren't born shuffling a deck of cards), and so on. With some of these unnatural sins, the urge to indulge may diminish or even disappear when we distance ourselves from them. But there is nothing we can do to escape things that come naturally, like food or sex. That's why our mouth waters for pizza or chocolate and why we feel drawn toward the forbidden charms of the opposite sex.

It is not sinful to crave food and sex. The sin comes when we indulge our innate drives in illegitimate ways or at illegitimate times. But what about illegitimate desires? Let's nail this down, all right? As long as we live and die here on this polluted planet, we must suffer the burning yearnings of perverted human nature. Don't feel guilty about them, don't give in to them, just ignore them and praise God for His peace and power in Jesus Christ.

Certainly there is much we can do to avoid temptation. Like exchanging thoughtless hours watching Johnny Carson for thoughtful time reading about Jesus in the Gospel of John. Finally the happy day will arrive when we see Jesus coming in the clouds of heaven. At that time He will transform our vile bodies "like unto his glorious body" (Phil. 3:21). Then these sinful bodies of death will be renewed with incorruptible purity. (See 1 Cor. 15:53.)

Important information here, don't you think? It could have spared me tons of teenage turmoil. Most of the adults in my church wore angel masks, reluctant to confess the slightest struggle to commit any sin worse than impatience. Such dishonesty took a terrible toll on us youth. Besieged as we were by temptation, we felt like wolves instead of sheep. Apparently God could have nothing to do with us until we reached the overripe age of 30, when all sinful desires ceased.

(Please understand that I'm not promoting public disclosure of specific sexual vulnerabilities. That would be disastrous, opening the door of temptation for unstable listeners. I'm just suggesting that we avoid leaving the false impression that Christians have holy flesh.)

Of course, once in a while the angel masks slipped, exposing the underlying hypocrisy. I think of a friend of mine from a different part of the country who spotted his pastor in the hospital gift shop—thumbing through a *Playboy* magazine. No, it couldn't be! He was a staunchly conservative preacher of righteousness who roundly condemned sin and sinners.

My friend quietly edged closer, afraid to learn the truth, yet curious to know. The pastor was tipping the magazine up and down so the light would not glaze his flesh-colored fantasy. A smile curled the edges of his lips.

As my friend witnessed all this, shock became disgust. He eventually dropped out of church. Such expression of human weakness was bad enough in a man of God. Hypocrisy was too much. I must say that no pastor of mine displayed moral laxity, nor did my academy teachers. They faithfully (yet futilely) worked to weed out our adolescent follies. "Young people, you must strive for perfection in Christ, or you will never be ready for Jesus to come," they warned. "Why be lost when salvation is free? You can't buy it, you can't work for it. The life-changing grace of God that perfects your life is free!"

Let me tell you, I came to the place where I wished salvation were *not* free. I wished I could sell my soul to God just so I could find relief from my tormenting conscience. But no, salvation was free. Elusively free beyond my grasp.

In the autumn of 1969, armed with my scholarships, I enrolled as a psychology major at Columbia Union College near Washington, D.C. It was a Christian school, but what did that matter anymore? Religion had become a nonevent in my life. I was burned out on God.

Too bad, Lord, I thought. *I really tried to serve You.*

The *Lineup* and the Letdown

4

WAR RAGED on the streets of Washington during my freshman year at college. Long-haired demonstrators battled short-tempered police, all in the name of peace in Vietnam.

As for my own little world, I still didn't have peace—but the war was over just the same. I had given up trying to please God. His life-changing grace was like moon dust. Free for the taking, but far beyond my grasp.

Since I couldn't go to heaven, I determined to enjoy life down here. Turmoil in Tranquility was behind me. I had a fresh start in a new environment where few knew my past history as a nerd. Why not play the part of a party animal?

I wasn't about to do anything foolish—no drinking or drugs or careless relationships. Just fun and lots of it. I would also study hard and graduate, marry a decent girl, and become a prosperous psychologist. I would even take my children to Capital Memorial church every week—perhaps somehow they would attain that spiritual pie in the sky which had eluded me.

Several weeks after fall registration, the college came out with the *Lineup*. This brown-covered booklet contained little mug shots of all the students. The appearance of the *Lineup* was a major event in the men's dorm, stimulating fervent discussions about the relative charms of the campus "chicks."

I retreated to my room, stretched out on my bed, and studied the photos. All those pretty faces seemed to be smiling at me. *And why not?* I mused. *I'm not "chubby Marty" anymore—I'm nearly six feet five now. Why can't I hold my own with the rest of the guys around here?*

So I shrugged off my old social insecurities and made a list of girls I wanted to date, then went to work. It's amazing how people tend to treat you exactly as you expect them to. Most of the girls I approached were happy to go out with me. One seemingly conceited little blonde spurned my advances. "Forget her," I sniffed. "She's too short for me anyway."

The girls I dated were decent though not too religious. We went to see *Romeo and Juliet, Easy Rider, Bonnie and Clyde*—not the worst movies, yet worldly just the same. I always insisted on taking my dates to church, too. That was my only concession to a worn-out conscience, along with paying tithe (I was afraid of robbing the Almighty). I had no delusions about salvation. I knew I wasn't saved. But since I was allergic to religion, salvation wasn't a reasonable consideration. If my soul couldn't be born again, at least my social life was.

So went my freshman year. Around November I decided I wanted to settle down with Lisa, a fellow freshman whose spiritual frustrations paralleled mine. She had the prettiest blue eyes I had ever seen. Her face even graced the cover of a national magazine. And beyond physical beauty she was tenderhearted.

The problem was that two other guys already liked her. They were formidable competition—both older than I, with money, and they were leaders in student government. For five bitter months the three of us battled it out. I prayed and prayed, "God, please grant my one request. Then I'll leave You alone."

I stopped at nothing to convince the girl of my dreams that I was her real Prince Charming. For instance, her mother was mildly annoyed by my New Jersey accent. Too unsophisticated, she thought, and Lisa agreed. No problem. I managed to deprogram my tongue remarkably quickly. To this day you wouldn't guess I'm from New Jersey.

Lisa loved art, so I tried to learn to paint. That didn't go so well, but she appreciated my effort. Lisa enjoyed chewing gum now and then. On her birthday I presented her a box with 365 individual sticks of gum, bundled by months, with each month labeled. Her birthday was February 17, as I recall, so the seventeenth stick of gum in February's bundle I wrapped with gold foil. Quite clever, I prided myself. She thought so too. It seemed I might be pulling ahead of my rivals.

Then I started getting up every morning at the unearthly hour of 5:00 to walk her to work at the Washington Adventist Hospital. My competitors were apparently still sleeping. "Dream on, you guys," I chortled as I splashed on English Leather.

In late March, when springtime begins blooming in Washington, love for me finally blossomed in Lisa's heart. She told the other fellows goodbye. I could hardly believe it. For the first time in my life I had a love relationship.

The passionate dawning of romantic love is the most intense pleasure in the world. Of course, what possessed me was more like selfish infatuation. Whatever it was, I didn't care—it felt a lot better than anything I had known before.

"Let the good times roll," I proclaimed. Even academic excellence was forgotten—Lisa was more fun than anything happening at the library. I sneaked my old white VW bug down from New Jersey. Freshmen back then weren't allowed to have cars on campus, probably a smart idea. I wasn't used to breaking rules, but I had to have some wheels for getting around with Lisa. Besides, where but in a car could we enjoy some privacy?

My fantasy springtime ushered in the long-awaited summer of love. I got a little apartment just down the street from the college. Hot, humid days gave way to evenings, time for fun.

The District of Columbia is a great place for lovers, and is still my favorite city in America. Lisa and I enjoyed rock concerts at Rock Creek Park, political barbecues at the Kennedy estate, and window-shopping at Prince George's Plaza.

However much I enjoyed all this, I still could find no peace or satisfaction within myself. Guilt and fear surged close to the surface of my consciousness. These feelings came into terrifying focus through a tragedy that summer. A college friend of mine, Jimmy, was brutally murdered one night in the woods behind the hospital. He had been a night watchman. Rumor had it that he might have known too much about the arson destruction the previous winter at Columbia Hall, one of the main buildings on campus. The police never solved Jimmy's murder (as far as I'm aware). All that I could think about for a few nights afterward was death. I jumped at every shadow—I knew I wasn't ready to die. Lisa was scared too.

That summer I had a job pumping gas at the world headquarters of the Seventh-day Adventist Church. The leaders were polite, all of them, but they couldn't think of much to say to the tousled teenager filling their tanks with Texaco Sky Chief. As time passed, though, several took an interest in me. George Vandeman, of the *It Is Written* telecast, (for whom I would work many years later) always had a pleasant word or two. And Roland Hegstad, editor of *Liberty* magazine, was always good for a friendly argument about religion and politics. Charles D. Brooks, my favorite Black preacher, never failed to deliver an encouraging word. More than anyone else, however, shuttle driver Joe Hillebert cheered my day.

Nobody knew that inside our desk at the gas station was a *Playboy* calendar. When I first saw it there, I cringed that my boss had the nerve to harbor such sin right there at church headquarters. *How could he bring ministers in here while hiding this around?* I worried. Fear and disgust couldn't stop me from taking occasional peeks at the luscious desecration, however.

What difference does it make? I told myself. *I'm lost anyway.* Thousands of religion-resistant young people raised in church feel exactly as I did then: "Why say no to sin if I'll never make it to heaven? What's the use of resisting temptation?"

Hopelessness is one of the devil's favorite tools. Many parents apparently don't realize that. They scold their teens with the straight testimony against sin to make them stop idolizing Madonna and Janet Jackson. But condemning worldliness isn't enough to inspire faith in Christ. Most of these kids are already burned out on religion. Frustrated by past failures, they long ago gave up hope and gave themselves over to sin. Hounding them about holiness only breeds perplexity and resentment. They need a gleam of hope that faith is within their grasp. "We are saved by hope" (Rom. 8:24).

An unexpected word of hope came to me one hot July afternoon at the station. I had just wiped the windshield for Elder Minchin, a dear old pastor soon to retire. I noticed him watching me. Then he stepped forward and put his arm on my shoulder. Looking me straight in the eye, he slowly announced, "Young man, the Lord has a great work for you someday."

That's all he said. Then the white-haired man of God got into his car and drove off. I stood there stunned. Hadn't the Lord forgotten me? But here was a word of hope—almost like some kind of prophecy! Then my heart sank. How could God want a confused young grease monkey who didn't even care anymore about a new heart?

Lisa and I always went to church, but all week long we lived only for each other. Although we never did everything there was to do, sexually speaking, we did a lot more than we should have. Then, feeling guilty, we would open the glove compartment of my VW and take turns reading a few paragraphs from *The Desire of Ages*, a book on the life of Christ.

Somehow we felt cleansed by reading that book, although we really weren't fooling ourselves. Both of us knew we were damned in the books of heaven.

Since we didn't have the Lord for a friend, the only thing that mattered to us was our growing relationship. One evening late in August we strolled through Sligo Creek Park, a place that holds many memories for me. We sat on the swings and talked a long time about our future. Yes, we really wanted to get married. We sealed our decision with a kiss. Talk about a magic moment!

Next morning, a Friday, I drove back to New Jersey to have my car inspected by the motor vehicle bureau. I couldn't wait to get back Sunday, flying down Interstate 95 as fast as my old VW could go. Exiting the beltway on University Boulevard, I could already feel Lisa's warm embrace.

When I knocked on her door, though, she wasn't waiting for me. Her mother's halfhearted greeting hinted that something was wrong. I roared off and finally located Lisa at her grandmother's place. She wasn't eager to talk, but I managed to get her outside.

"What's the matter with you tonight?" I demanded.

"You don't really want to know," she replied, staring down at the curb. "I still like you as a friend, but . . ."

"What! What are you saying?"

Her eyes glistened in the glare of the street lamp. "You and I—we're through. Last night one of the guys I used to know dropped by. He convinced me I'm too young to settle down with you. I want to date around again."

I began to protest, and then caught myself. "You really mean it, don't you?" I asked, not daring to accept reality.

35

She bit her lip. "Yes, I really do."

I felt as though I might faint. My lanky frame crumpled into the car. She leaned against the roof and looked inside. "I'm really sorry, Marty. I didn't think it would turn out like this. I hope we can still be good friends."

Good friends indeed! Maybe even pen pals.

Hot tears swirled in my eyes as I started the car. I managed to drive home and creep upstairs to my decrepit apartment.

So much for my summer of love. No more love songs and promises. We had only just begun, yet now we were through. I might have ended it all that night, really, but I didn't have the nerve to slit my wrists. And there weren't any pills around on which to overdose.

Next day the cruel sunlight awakened me. Splashing cold water on my puffy eyes, I reminded myself that what happened wasn't just a nightmare. It was really true. Lisa and I were through.

All that morning I hid behind the gas station, crouched between green and white Texaco oil drums. When a car pulled in I wiped my eyes, emerged to pump gas, then retreated to cry some more. At noontime it hit me—this was stupid. Might as well move on with life. She wanted to date around. Well, so could I.

But no, I couldn't. I just didn't have the heart to go out with anyone else. So I sat in my room and waited for my sophomore year to start. Bored and lonely, I turned to an old friend of mine, ice cream. One night I ate a whole half gallon of Safeway's finest Peaches 'n' Cream.

Life was anything but a peach when, several days before registration, the engine blew out on my VW. Since I had full responsibility for my college bill beyond the scholarships, I couldn't afford to fix it. In desperation I phoned my father for help. He agreed to buy me a new engine—on one condition. I would have to promise him to read every day from a book he handed me. It was the daily devotional book published by my own church.

"Fair enough," I replied, thinking to myself, *Not a bad deal! For a $600 engine job I'll read a few words every night from this little blue book.*

In the weeks ahead I kept my promise, just barely, reading only a sentence or two before twisting off the lamp beside my bed. Then, as I squirmed in the darkness, those few words I had read stirred up old familiar fears of damnation. "I'm lost! Jesus is coming soon, and I am lost!"

Just as the guilt began to get out of hand, another Week of Prayer rolled around. *Well, Lord,* I thought, *are You ready to try again with me?*

Free at Last?

5

IT'S GOT to be now or never, Lord!"
I could hardly believe it. Here I was trying to get spiritual again. Not that I held much hope for success—my chances were about one in 10 of ever making it to heaven, I figured. But I had to give religion another try. Nothing else was working.

"*Please*, Lord," I pleaded, "teach me how to be a Christian!" But God sent no answers. And the people I sought counsel from simply recycled the same pious platitudes that had confused me in the first place.

Just when I was nearing the end of my hope, the time arrived for the autumn Week of Prayer at Columbia Union College. My friends considered the speaker somewhat boring; he didn't dazzle us with star-spangled stories. But in his plain-Jane presentations I heard a message of hope as never before in my life.

Monday morning he quoted a special promise from deep inside the Old Testament: "And you will seek Me and find Me, when you search for Me with all your heart" (Jer. 29:13, NKJV). It was the very text I needed to keep hanging on to for hope—if I would search for God with all my heart, I would finally find Him. He promised!

Carefully I listened as the speaker explained heaven's facts of life. I had always known that Jesus died for my sins, a gift received by some mysterious quality known as faith. Now for the first time I learned what faith really meant.

Faith isn't some exclusive quality limited to spiritual giants. *It's simply the willingness to exchange what the world offers for what God offers us in Christ.* First we exchange our guilt for His forgiveness. We also exchange our weakness for His strength. Finally we exchange our own way of doing things for God's will.

That's faith, pure and simple, faith that brings salvation.

Carried forth into daily living, this same exchange (of what the world offers us for what God offers us in Christ) nurtures Christian growth.

Seems clear enough, I thought, *but how do I learn to exercise this faith? How do I make this practical?*

I set up an appointment with the speaker to find out. He shared a verse that unlocked the secret of faith. "Let us fix our eyes on Jesus, the author and perfecter of our faith" (Heb. 12:2, NIV).

"But I can't see Jesus!" I protested.

"He's in His Word, the Bible," the speaker assured me. "There we see Him forgiving all kinds of sinners—thieves, prostitutes, headstrong disciples, and even proud Pharisees. It dawns on us that the same mercy and power He had for sinners back then He still has for us today. His love softens our hearts and makes us want to live for Him."

"Sounds sensible," I said hopefully as I headed off to class. Christianity had always seemed so complicated, always obsessed with attaining instant sinlessness. Now I learned to trust Christ's accomplishments instead of my own spiritual achievements.

That night as I turned out the light I kept wondering, *Is all this really true? Can God really look upon me and say, "You are My beloved son, in whom I am well pleased"?*

"No!" my conscience snarled. "God can't smile at you. He's got His eyebrows raised until you overcome every sin. You don't deserve His approval yet."

Then the thought occurred—Did Jesus deserve what He got on the cross? Certainly not. Well, then, if He didn't deserve what He got (my guilt), then I need not deserve what I get (God's approval). *Christ got what I deserve so that I can get what He deserves.* He wore my crown of thorns so that I can wear His eternal crown of glory.

There in the friendly darkness of my room I prayed, "Lord, I love what You offer me in Christ. It's so much better than the foolish counterfeits I had before. I want to worship You forever!"

Like a starving man discovering a feast, I began getting up early to study all I could about faith. From its many uses throughout Scripture, certain facts began to emerge. Faith is not the absence of doubt, but the decision to cling to God's promises despite doubt and confusion. Faith is not the absence of fear, but a dogged determination to trust God despite our fears. And faith isn't the absence of guilty feelings, but the hanging of our helpless souls on the cross of Christ despite being bombarded by guilt.

Some of this I learned right away, and some of it took years to really understand. The best news to me was that I could consider myself a Christian even before overcoming my sins.

Wow! I thought. *I'm accepted in Christ despite my struggle with Nestle's Crunch bars! If I happen to gobble four of them in one sitting, God still doesn't cast me off as a lost soul!* Of course, I knew He would also begin working to develop in me a character that would bring Him glory. And such a lifestyle would eventually include some appetite control over candy bars.

Well, at last I understood the ABCs of the gospel, at the age of 18. When the speaker made an altar call at the end of the Week of Prayer, I jumped out of the pew and strode up the aisle of that huge church, publicly surrendering my life to God. Many times before, I had made such a commitment, ever so sincerely, but now for the first time I would truly trust Christ for my salvation.

The date was October 3, 1970. I'll always remember that Friday night in Sligo Adventist Church when I sealed my decision for Jesus. I grabbed a white response card and signed my name. Then I wrote a P.S. echoing the triumphant declaration of the late Martin Luther King, Jr.: "Thank God, I'm free at last!" As I stepped outside the church into the chilly autumn air, God's acceptance warmed my heart. I could hardly believe it—free at last, happily ever after with Jesus.

Not quite. The battle had only just begun. It's amazing how you can learn the truth in your mind, but your emotions still believe the old lies. This confusion necessitates what the Bible calls the "fight of faith."

The morning after I took my stand for Christ I woke up feeling unworthy again. That same old rotten guilt! As I slowly slid over the side of the bed to my knees, I had quite a struggle believing that my prayer was going to make it higher than the dormitory ceiling.

I found myself still confusing peaceful *feelings* with the *fact* of forgiveness we have in Jesus. In so many ways, feelings often fool us. I remember feeling awful about a scholastic aptitude test I had taken in high school—until I got notice that it had qualified me for a scholarship. Sometimes feelings work the other way, too. My friend down the hall felt great about the chemistry test he said he aced—until he got his D. Spiritually, too, feelings often fail to tell the truth. We might feel guilt-stricken even after we have entrusted ourselves to Christ and all is well with our soul. Or we might feel confident about heaven while yet in an unrepentant, unsaved state.

Like clouds crossing a sunny sky, feelings come and go. Firm commitment based on trust is the anchor that secures any relationship, including our relationship with God. So "if our heart condemns us, God is greater than our heart, and knows all things" (1 John 3:20, NKJV). He knows we have indeed accepted Jesus Christ, and all remains well with our soul no matter how guilty we might feel.

This lesson served me well a few weeks after becoming a Christian. As I closed my Bible one November morning and got dressed for my 7:00 math class, a troubling thought began gnawing at my conscience: *Was I losing some of my appreciation for Jesus that I had when first forgiven?* All day long I worried, *Am I losing it, Lord? Have I gotten too comfortable in Christ, taking Him for granted now?*

That evening I decided to talk it over with Bob Jones, a fellow classmate and my favorite spiritual adviser. When I knocked at his second-floor room, I could hear him strumming a psalm on his guitar. He finished his song for me and then listened as I spilled out my frustration.

Bob smiled. "Nothing's wrong, Marty. Relationships go through stages—all of them do. The 'honeymoon' stage is great while it lasts, but it sure enough ends sooner or later. Some of that feeling fades away, even while love is growing. Here's what's important—maintain your commitment to the relationship. Do whatever you can to nurture it. You know, with prayer and study, fellowship and witnessing, too." Then he reassured me with a smile. "I'm keeping an eye on you, Marty. You're doing just fine."

Good old Bob. Thank God for his spiritual tow truck. Still

one of my closest friends 20 years later, he pastors a church in San Diego.

The first dramatic test of my Christian experience came later that November. I returned to my dorm room one day after lunch and threw down my books on the desk. What was that I smelled? Something familiar—my favorite perfume! I turned around, and there by the door was Lisa.

"How in the world did you sneak up here?" I demanded. Without waiting for her answer, I fled the room and headed outside. She followed me down the back stairs to a park bench near the center of the campus. Whatever was going to happen, at least it would be out in the open.

"Marty," she sobbed, "I made a terrible mistake. I want you back. Please love me again."

A thousand ropes pulled at my heart. But I had a new love in my life to which I had to be faithful.

"Lisa," I replied as tenderly as I could without letting her charms lure me away. "I still care about you, but there's no way I'm going back to that disordered, destructive relationship we had. I don't know if you can relate to what I'm saying, but please try to understand."

She didn't understand. I forced myself to walk away. It wasn't easy.

How things had changed in the last year! The previous November I would have sacrificed everything in the world to win Lisa's love. Now she felt exactly that way about me. But I had discovered something better than the old relationship we had, something more enduring and satisfying—a relationship with Christ.

Lisa had done wonders for my sense of self-worth. She had chosen me above my rivals and welcomed me as her life partner. That made me feel special indeed. But then she broke up with me, and my little world collapsed. The love of Jesus would never let me down like that.

Many times I've wondered if I should have tried to help Lisa find Jesus that afternoon at the park. Perhaps, though, I had to be firm—almost unfeeling. I had to keep my feelings from sweeping me back to her charms.

Several months later I called Lisa and invited her to meet me in the Upper Room, a little haven set apart for meditation on the third floor of the campus center. We greeted each other, shook hands, and sat down in separate velvet armchairs. Both of us felt strange with each other. In a short time we had grown far apart. Things relaxed when I started talking about the big change in my life.

"Lisa, believe me, life with Jesus is better than anything I knew before—even the good times we used to enjoy. I've got something solid to live for now. You know, purpose and meaning, and all that. Peace with God makes all the difference in the world." Then I paused before adding, "I've still got struggles, plenty of them, but I know God's on my side. And even on those bad days I can remind myself that heaven will be better than anything we know down here."

"Wouldn't you like to know Jesus too?" I reached toward her hand pleadingly, then caught myself and drew back.

Lisa was obviously impressed by the new me. Her longing eyes filled with tears. "I admire what you've got, Marty, and I wish I had it too," she said haltingly, pitifully. Moments passed in silence, her head bowed. Then she stiffened abruptly. "I'm just not ready to make the big commitment."

With that, she rose to leave. We shook hands again and she was gone. The lingering shadows of late afternoon streaked across the Upper Room as I sat quietly praying for her. I don't know if she ever did accept Jesus. With that tender heart of hers, I like to think she did.

As for me, God managed to keep me from returning to the old life. Temptations from the flesh still haunted me, sure enough. But my toughest battle was always with my torturing conscience. The devil continually attacked me through some pious guilt trip, seeking to discourage me from trusting in God's mercy.

Frequently I stubbed my toe on some troublesome text. Like 1 John 3:9, which declares in the King James Version: "Whosoever is born of God doth not commit sin . . . and he cannot sin, because he is born of God."

Ouch! Does that mean that if we're not perfect, then we're not born again?

"Not at all," my friend Bob Jones assured me. He blamed

my perplexity on a deficient translation of this text in the normally accurate (though archaic) King James Version. "First John 3:9 is really saying that for Christians, sin is not our chosen lifestyle. *The New American Standard Bible* reflects this true meaning: 'No one who is born of God practices sin.' Of course, even the most faithful Christians 'fall short of the glory of God' [Rom. 3:23, NKJV]. But there is a difference between chasing after sin—as people of the world do—and running away from sin, as a Christian does. That's why the Bible says 'there is therefore now no condemnation to those who are in Christ Jesus, who do not walk according to the flesh, but according to the Spirit' [Rom. 8:1, NKJV]."

Well, once again my mind was at peace, and I continued to grow in the Lord. As I learned more about Jesus, an old question came to mind about who He really is. My father had insisted that Christ was a created being who had visited earth as something of a super angel. I think he picked that up from the Jehovah's Witnesses. On the other hand, my religion teachers at college taught that Jesus was God in human flesh, the eternal Lord of glory.

Who was right? I had to find out. One Saturday night I lugged my big blue concordance and my Bible to the Upper Room. Alone in my favorite refuge, I determined to learn the truth about Jesus. My search began in the Gospel of John. "In the beginning was the Word, and the Word was with God, and the Word was God. . . . All things were made through Him. . . . And the Word became flesh and dwelt among us" (John 1:1, 3, 14, NKJV). So Jesus, called the Word, is indeed God. Does this mean He is the same as God the Father? No, because Jesus said, "I do not seek My own will but the will of the Father who sent Me" (John 5:30, NKJV).

Jesus didn't have a split personality. Evidently He and the Father are distinct persons, members together along with the Holy Spirit of the Godhead mentioned in Colossians 2:9. They are something like a marriage unit, only with three members instead of two.

I also discovered that the One born in Bethlehem existed beforehand, even "from the days of eternity" (Micah 5:2, NASB). Then why is Jesus called "Son of God," since He is an eternal member of the Godhead? Luke 1:35 put into place that piece of the puzzle: "And the angel answered and said to her [Mary], 'The Holy Spirit will come upon you, and the power of the Highest will overshadow you; therefore, also, that Holy One who is to be born will be called the Son of God' " (Luke 1:35, NKJV).

"I get it!" I almost shouted. "Jesus is the 'Son of God' because He was born of the virgin Mary—not because He was a created being." "Son of God" meant He was different from every other son born to human parents—He alone is divine.

It was late that Saturday night before I closed my Bible, satisfied that I had found the truth about Jesus Christ. Before I left the Upper Room I did something special. For the first time in my life I fell on my knees before Jesus and worshiped Him as Lord. Words can't describe what an experience that was.

That Saturday night in the Upper Room was only the beginning of many exciting treasure hunts in God's Word. Encouraged by the prayers and fellowship of friends like Bob Jones, I dug my spiritual foundations deep. It was a good thing I did, because of the adventure awaiting me in Pennsylvania that summer.

Adventure in Pennsylvania

6

IN FEBRUARY of 1971 the makers of Rolls Royce automobiles declared bankruptcy and were quickly rescued by the British government. The old VW that I drove wasn't quite a Rolls Royce, but at least I didn't have a problem going bankrupt. Long hours as a janitor supplemented my scholarships in subduing my college bill. I was surviving spiritually as well.

In fact, I was thriving. Having made it through my first winter safe and sound in Jesus, I dedicated my life to sharing His good news. My friend Bob Jones took me along on evangelistic Bible studies. I enjoyed that so much I volunteered to spend a year as a student missionary. Some of my friends had returned with glowing testimonies after serving on some exotic island in the South Pacific or way up in the Yukon Territory of Canada. I craved the same experience.

Night by night while drifting off to sleep I pictured myself wearing one of those big white missionary hats and teaching hundreds of eager people. I could hardly wait to get to Borneo—or wherever.

Then came the big letdown. The mission board turned me down—I wasn't going to Borneo or anyplace else.

Upperclassmen had priority, it seemed. That was only fair, but you can imagine my disappointment. And the uncertainty—I wondered just what it was God wanted me to do that coming summer. My friends Ray and Bill came up with a plan. They suggested that I do door-to-door witnessing, selling *Bible Story* books (the ones you see in doctors' offices).

"No thanks," I told them. "I'm no salesman." That much I knew from experience. Shortly after becoming a Christian, I had tried selling those same *Bible Story* books. No matter how I prayed and tried my best, people refused to let me in their house. I sold nothing—zero. I had to quit.

Ray and Bill thought I needed another chance. Right about

that time the literature evangelist leaders from the mid-Atlantic states came to the college to recruit students for summer colporteur work. Their task was about as challenging as recruiting soldiers for Vietnam.

I knew of some students before my time who pulled a nasty prank on a colporteur recruiter. One of them, posing as a bright prospect, told the recruiter he wanted to discuss selling books that summer. They agreed to meet after supper in the lobby of the dorm. Meanwhile, the pranksters wired up one of the lobby chairs to a large battery so that when two wires were touched, a harmless but startling shock was administered to the seat of the victim.

The bait set, at the appointed hour the pretended prospect met the unsuspecting recruiter and escorted him to the hot seat. His accomplice hid behind a couch, wires in hand. Throughout the earnest discussion about working for the Lord, the poor recruiter couldn't stop himself from jumping up and down in his chair.

"What's the matter, Elder?" the student inquired ever so innocently.

"Nothing, really. I guess my nerves are just acting up."

It was those fellows who had the nerve acting up like that. Yet even the colporteur leader himself thought it was somewhat funny when he later learned the truth about his hot seat.

I had no desire to play tricks on the colporteur recruiters; I just wanted them to pass me by. So I spent a lot of time that week hiding in the library. Just confronting the recruiters would have been much better, but I hadn't yet learned how to do that. Back then I found it easier to hide from people who were trying to persuade me about something on which I had already made up my mind.

"Why should I make a bankrupt fool of myself trying to sell books?" I reasoned. "Surely God has something different in mind for me."

The recruiters were hot on my trail—someone had given them my name. All week long I managed to evade them. That was no easy accomplishment, since they had even staked out the cafeteria. (I ate in the snack bar.) Their last chance to get me was Thursday night at worship. I sat in the back waiting to make my escape to the library after closing prayer.

The moment I heard "Amen" I bolted for the door. Not quickly enough, though. My friends Ray and Bill yelled for me to stop, and sure enough, there with them was the colporteur leader of the Pennsylvania Conference.

"Marty!" he exclaimed. "I've been looking for you all week. They tell me you want to sell books this summer, and I've got just the territory for you."

I glared at Ray and Bill, who grinned back at me. I could have bumped their heads together!

"Don't worry about a thing," the leader continued reassuringly, undeterred by my underwhelming enthusiasm. "I've even found a room for you to stay at a pastor's house—his wife bakes the best homemade bread. Now, here's a map with your territory. Work begins a week after classes let out."

"Thanks a lot," I murmured, attempting a smile. Despite my dismay over this unwelcome development, I didn't want to rule out the possibility of God's leading. Besides, it felt good to be wanted. So I promised to pray about my decision.

I believed then, as now, that God has a plan for our lives. This plan was in place before we were even born, according to Psalm 139. And no matter what mistakes we have made in the past, the Lord is well able to work out all things for good and guide us now.

But, I wondered, *how can I be certain of His will? How can I know what He wants me to do this summer?*

I found some help in Proverbs 3:5, 6: "Trust in the Lord with all your heart, and do not lean on your own understanding. In all your ways acknowledge Him, and He will make your paths straight" (NASB).

I saw three conditions there for receiving God's guidance: First, "trust in the Lord," that is, I must rely on God by faith for all my needs. Next, "do not lean on your own understanding"—I must accept that God's way might go against my own ideas, my own wisdom (like being a student missionary in Borneo). Then the final condition: "In all your ways acknowledge Him." In other words, I should accept His leadership in every aspect of my life. That made sense. How could I expect guidance from God unless I was willing to acknowledge His total lordship of my life?

Perhaps the biggest barrier to knowing God's will is a stubborn attitude. Jesus said, "If any man is willing to do His [God's] will, he shall know" (John 7:17, NASB). So if I wanted to know God's will, I had to be willing to consider all options, including selling books in Pennsylvania. I reluctantly told the Lord I would go wherever He sent me.

Having met the conditions of God's guidance as best as I knew how, I could confidently claim that promise: "He will make your paths straight."

Would I hear an angel's voice in the middle of the night? Probably not. Never In more than 20 years of Christian service have I ever heard a literal voice from God or seen an angel. Never has God guided me by spectacular revelations of His will. Instead, God has unfailingly guided my life by impressing my mind or quietly opening doors of opportunity—often working through the ideas of friends or sometimes even the wrath of enemies. I can look back now and realize how He has definitely fulfilled His plan for me.

Sounds good, you may be thinking. *But what if I somehow miss the Lord's signals when He tries to guide me?*

Nothing to worry about there. When we sincerely commit ourselves to God, it's *His* business to make His will plain to us. He somehow manages to reveal His will just when the time is right. He can work through us, beyond us, and even in spite of us to fulfill His purposes. And by the way, His will turns out to be just what we would choose for ourselves if we knew the end from the beginning.

Well, obviously God didn't want me to be a student missionary in Borneo, since that door had slammed shut. My mother suggested I find a job near her apartment in New Jersey, but nothing available there afforded me opportunity for full-time evangelism. Perhaps this Pennsylvania idea wasn't so bad. Maybe it really was God's will. Since every other option was either impossible or impractical, I decided to sell the books.

I'll never forget the lonely feeling as I drove my little white VW west on Interstate 80 toward Indiana County, Pennsylvania. The majestic mountains along the way only made me feel insignificant and isolated. There was lots of time for reflection during that 300-mile trip. I analyzed my previous failure in selling the

Bible Story books. My intentions were fine, but I had no business trying to master sales skills while burdened with an overload of college studies. I should have stuck with being a janitor—physical work provided a break from mentally taxing studies.

Another reason my sales attempt fizzled was that I didn't memorize my presentations. I just "trusted" Jesus to take over and sell the books through me. Someone had counseled me to do that. "Just go out there with prayer in your heart, and Jesus will do the rest."

Well, He didn't. Now I understand that there is no such thing as "letting go and letting Jesus" work, as if Christianity offered some kind of spiritual cruise control. That's not the way the Christian life works. God's Word has a lot to say about effort. It takes effort to get up in the morning to spend time with Jesus. It takes effort when temptation comes to turn to God for help. God gives strength, but we must trust Him for it. That's not always easy. It certainly wasn't easy taking up my post in Pennsylvania. I determined to thoroughly memorize my sales talks and dozens of God's promises.

My first day of selling dawned sunny and warm. I drove to Blairsville to meet Paul, my supervisor, who would break me in that day. We found a neighborhood with children's toys scattered around (known to salesmen as "kiddy litter") and set off going door-to-door. People responded to Paul's skills. By late afternoon he had sold a set of *The Bible Story* and some books for adults.

This isn't going to be hard at all, I thought. *I can do this quite well by myself.*

Just about then a cloud began to cover me. Not a cloud from the sky, but a cloud over my mind—a cloud of discouragement smothering my faith, invisible but just as real as London pea soup fog. I simply couldn't go on.

"Paul, I have to stop. Let me go back to the car."

"Why?"

"I—I can't explain it. I just feel I can't do this all summer. I've got to quit."

In the car Paul opened his Bible and read, while I sat there smothered in gloom. What was happening to me? After 10 minutes or so Paul looked up. "Well, Marty, what are we going to do?"

"I think I should go home," I mumbled.

"Instead of that, why don't we claim God's promise here in Psalm 27:14—'Wait on the Lord, be of good courage, and He will strengthen your heart' " (NKJV).

Paul wanted to pray, so I bowed my head. Nothing happened when we prayed—I felt as depressed as ever. But as we stepped out of the car to go back to work, that cloud somehow lifted. I can't explain it, but instantly my midnight became like noontime. Full of God's joy, we strode to the next door and sold a set of books. I never looked back the rest of the summer.

When God let me suffer that fog and then took it away, I think He was teaching me my absolute helplessness. Only through His sustaining strength could I work for Him. God also showed me the importance of stepping out by faith without feeling. Not until I got out of the car to go back to work did my cloud go away.

Nothing like that experience has ever happened to me since. Many times I've had to plow ahead under miserable circumstances, yet the Lord has somehow seen me through it all.

Often people pray that God will take away their doubts. I think it's a mistake to pray a lot about our doubts and fears. Faith is not the absence of doubt and fear but our clinging to God despite negative emotions. We must thank Him for the invisible power of His Holy Spirit and simply move ahead obeying His will. Strength comes when we trust and obey.

My big test on this point came the second day of work. Paul had to move on, leaving me all by myself on a cloudy day. As I drove south on Highway 119 it started to drizzle.

"I don't need this, Lord," I complained, imagining myself slinking from door-to-door like a wet house cat. I drove on, eventually finding myself in Lucerne Mines, a mining town with several streets of little houses filthy with coal dust. Several snarling dogs greeted my arrival. Sort of a depressing place to start work.

"Help me," I prayed, forcing myself out of the car. As I walked up to the first house, I noticed that the drizzle had stopped. All day long I trudged from house to house through power not my own. I even sold a book. I was so happy that when the lady handed me her check, I reached down to pet her little chihuahua. "You cute baby!" I exclaimed, and the ugly beast bit me. Thanks a lot!

Really, I didn't mind that much. A dog bite was a worthy trade-off for selling my first book. I left that house holding my finger and praising the Lord.

Another dog bite that summer was harder to take. It happened one afternoon in early June. I thought God was impressing me to leave the neighborhood I was working and go back to a house where the day before nobody had been home. I remembered hearing about a literature evangelist who had felt impressed to stop what he was doing and visit a house—just in time to save a woman from committing suicide. Would something like that happen to me?

It took a while to sift through rush-hour traffic, but at last I pulled up to my house of destiny and knocked on the door. At first it seemed nobody was home. I kept knocking. Still no answer.

Bitterly disappointed, I turned to leave. Just then, from the corner of my eye I saw him coming. He ran right up to me and bit my leg. Not only did that stupid dog ruin a nice pair of slacks; he also bit off a big chunk of my faith.

Why, Lord? I still haven't figured it all out, though one lesson was immediately obvious—sincere impressions of God's will can be mistaken.

The Bible presents a God more eager to give us good things than we are to ask for them. In light of that, I learned not to make my love for God dependent upon answered prayer—also, not to doubt His love for me when He doesn't give me what I hope for. More than that, I learned not to question my salvation if my faith doesn't seem to get my prayers answered.

I learned other things about prayer. Its purpose isn't to get God to do things our way; it enables us to do things His way. If God gave us everything we wanted or thought we needed, prayer would only pander to our ignorance and selfishness —not an uplifting experience at all. The deepest goal in prayer is fostering our fellowship with God, deepening our relationship with Him.

Well, that summer in Pennsylvania I really got acquainted with the Lord. It was a difficult and lonely assignment that I never really learned to enjoy. Through it all, however, I felt a lot more fulfilled and satisfied than during my previous "summer of love" with Lisa. For me, selling books was something like boot camp for the Marines—tough but rewarding. When I dropped exhausted into bed at night, I knew I was right where God wanted me. I was doing His will.

The morning of June 30 I committed my life to Him as usual, not realizing that it would nearly end that evening.

The Day My Children Almost Died

7

THE DAY I almost died dawned clear and warm. Before 10:00 that morning the heat was sweltering. By noon my shirt was so soaked with sweat it looked like I had run through somebody's lawn sprinklers—a tempting thought as I trudged from house to house. My prospective customers were too hot and bothered even to look at my books, much less buy them. I could hardly get anyone to give me a glass of water. Only the neighborhood dogs responded to my presence, barking incessantly at my wilted form lugging that heavy brown case of books.

Although nobody bought that day, the Lord had plentifully blessed my sales so far that summer. By this, the last day of June, I was well on my way toward earning whatever college expenses my scholarships didn't cover. So it was more a sense of duty than necessity that sustained my lonely journey through purgatory that afternoon.

Evening brought relief. I had a couple Bible studies lined up, so I tossed my bookcase in the back seat and bade goodbye to all those grouchy housewives and their snarling dogs. I revved up my car and roared off. Unfortunately, I got to my first study a few minutes late, and my none-too-eager student had already left to go shopping. Just my day!

Angry with myself and with him, I sipped some water from a well and cooled off under a tree. Then, glancing at my watch, I jumped in my car and raced off toward Homer City for my next Bible study. The appointment was with a busy pastor, and I determined not to be late for him.

So there I was, speeding along a narrow country road. Suddenly, while rounding a sharp curve, I saw a big silver Buick lunging toward me. A head-on collision was imminent. Horrified, I steered hard to the right, missing the Buick but smashing into a dirt embankment. My VW spun around and began somersaulting. The door flung open and the spinning vehicle tossed me outside. I hit the blacktop, sliding on my back, my car bouncing along beside me. I finally came to rest with the car upside down an arm's length away.

I staggered to my feet, completely unharmed except for cuts on my back. The driver of the Buick and a nearby farmer ran to help me. Together we rolled the smashed car over and pushed it off the road. Then they stood there and stared at me as if I were a ghost from the cemetery.

The farmer insisted on loading me into his pickup truck for a ride to the hospital, where the doctors kept me overnight for observation. The next morning my brother Bill arrived in his black VW and took me home to New Jersey. After a week of rest, I bought an old turquoise Ford and headed back to finish off my Pennsylvania adventure.

The only reminders of that awful accident are scars on my back and some slivers of glass still inside. I also have some books that were mangled when they flew out the door with me and were smashed by the tumbling car.

How I survived that nightmare of broken glass and twisted metal, God only knows. But I almost died that day at the age of 19—and my two children almost died as well.

Wait a minute, you might be wondering. *You already had two kids at that tender age?*

Well, they weren't born yet. Then how was it that they almost died? To understand what I mean, it will help to think about George Washington. Had the father of America drowned the winter night he crossed the icy Delaware on his way to Valley Forge, twentieth-century America would have died with its founding father—just as my unborn children would have lost their opportunity for life had I been killed in my accident.

The ancient actions of our ancestors affect us yet today. The seed they sowed yields a harvest that generations yet unborn must reap, for better or worse. In a very real sense, what happened to them long ago actually happened to us as well.

This insight may be new to us, but we find it in the Bible. Did you know that Levi got credit for something his great-grandfather Abraham did many years previously? God considered unborn Levi a tithepayer because Abraham had been faithful with his tithe: "Even Levi, who receives tithes, paid tithes through Abraham, so to speak" (Heb. 7:9, NKJV).

Verse 10 explains: "For he [Levi] was still in the loins of his father [Abraham]" (NKJV). So unborn Levi was "in Abraham" when Abraham fulfilled the law, and thus by accepting God's covenant with Abraham he received credit for his ancestor's obedience. This intriguing reality illustrates an essential truth that concerns the whole human race—what it means for us to be "in Adam" or "in Christ."

According to the Bible, all of us died many centuries ago: "Having concluded this, that one died for all, therefore *all died*" (2 Cor. 5:14, NASB). The whole human race died together. We died twice, in fact—first in the Garden of Eden when Adam sinned, then later at the cross with Christ.

Let's probe deeper: "Therefore, just as through one man sin entered into the world, and death through sin, and so death spread to all men, because all sinned" (Rom. 5:12, NASB). Intriguing indeed. The Bible says "all sinned" with Adam, back there in the Garden of Eden. And because of it, we all met our death 6,000 years ago.

"But that's not fair," we protest. "Why should God let us suffer blame for something we never did?" Well, it wouldn't be fair if He expected us to remedy Adam's fall ourselves. But He sent Jesus to reconcile this world, replacing condemnation with justification. Notice verse 18: "So then as through one transgression there resulted condemnation to all men, even so through one act of righteousness there resulted justification of life to all men" (NASB).

What happened to us at Calvary counteracts what happened to us in Eden. We were "in Adam" when he sinned and brought condemnation upon the entire human family. But thank God, we also were "in Christ" when He brought salvation to "all men."

This brings us to an important question: If these events happened to us beyond our control, what about personal freedom of choice?

Freedom to choose is restored through the gospel. We have our choice of parents—Adam or Christ, along with our choice of history—Adam's sin or Christ's salvation. We can even choose our verdict in the judgment—Adam's condemnation or Christ's justification.

So what happened to us at Calvary more than atoned for what happened to us in Eden. Justification of life came upon "all men"—yet not everyone will be saved. Only those who "*receive* the abundance of grace and of the gift of righteousness" (Rom. 5:17, NASB). Justification and condemnation —both are historical facts already accomplished. All we can do is accept one or the other. I now understand that my spiritual successes don't save me, nor do my spiritual failures disqualify me. I was lost 6,000 years ago in Eden and then reconciled 2,000 years ago at Calvary. *Salvation depends upon which event of my past I choose to put my faith into.* My death in Adam will doom me. My death and new life in Jesus will save me.

Reconciliation with God is an accomplished fact. "God was in Christ reconciling the world to Himself" (2 Cor. 5:19, NKJV). The question today is not Can I be saved? but Do I want to accept the salvation already achieved in Christ?

This gospel that assures my salvation also provides unimagined possibilities for character development. Not only did Jesus conquer the penalty of sin at Calvary; He also conquered its power. The question now is not Can I be victorious? but Do I want to accept my victory already achieved in Christ?

Let me tell you about a fellow I knew during my summer in Pennsylvania. I'll call him Bob. A ministerial student, he served in a territory not far from mine. Bob was a truly converted believer but with one big weakness. Whenever sales did not measure up to his prayerful expectations, he felt sure something was wrong with his faith. That left him discouraged, imagining himself alienated from God. Dark thoughts churned within his mind: *What's the use? Why am I resisting the temptations around me if I'm spiritually hopeless anyway?*

His faith paralyzed by guilt, Bob would sneak in the side door of the drugstore downtown and buy a pornographic magazine. An hour later his conscience condemned him all the more. In disgust he tore up the offensive magazine and burned it. Then he would repent with many tears, feel forgiven, and eventually go about the Lord's work again.

Certainly Bob had no excuse for his sin, and he would be the first to agree. He knew what the Bible says: "Are we to continue in sin that grace might increase? May it never be! How shall we who died to sin still live in it?" (Rom. 6:1, 2, NASB).

Sin's power ended at the cross. Victory over temptation is our spiritual birthright in Christ—never again need we yield to temptation. "Even so consider yourselves to be dead to sin, but alive to God in Christ Jesus" (verse 11, NASB).

Notice that our death to sin is not something that *we* accomplish when we repent. We died at the cross, remember? Now we simply accept our death in Christ and claim the resurrection victory we have already won in Him.

But does that mean Bob wasn't a genuine Christian because he failed sometimes in fulfilling Christ's victory? His own conscience denounced him as a hypocrite unfit to bear witness for His Lord. I tried to help him see that hypocrites are phonies who refuse to forsake hidden sin while pretending to be righteous. Jesus reserved His stunning denunciations for those pious impostors who condemned sinners while secretly indulging in the same behavior. As for human weakness like Bob's, our Lord showed tender mercy.

Bob finally learned to trust the mercy of God, and that brought him strength in overcoming temptation. I saw him again recently for the first time in many years. He had been overseas as a missionary and now has a thriving ministry here in the States.

Well, so much for Bob. Satan has two great traps for us, the goal of both being the same—separating ourselves from what Christ has already accomplished. First, the enemy wants us to live in the flesh, indulging in Adam's failure as though we never died to the power of sin in Christ. Every true believer yearns to be free from all indulgence in sin, living out the victorious life Jesus already won for us.

Now, once we escape that first trap of indulging ourselves in Adam's fallen nature, the devil baits us with another one. He tempts us to compete with our righteous record already established by the perfection of Christ's obedience. Remember, we are not saved by our spiritual successes or lost by our failures.

Just as Levi fulfilled the law "in Abraham," so we already fulfilled the law "in Christ." Today we accept that righteous record—we don't compete with it.

What, then, is the purpose of character development if not to earn us a ticket to heaven? To glorify God, Jesus said: "Let your light so shine before men, that they may see your good works, and glorify your Father which is in heaven" (Matt. 5:16). By participating in God's transforming power, we bring glory to His name. And when we enjoy the security of God's acceptance in Christ, overcoming sin is not a threat but an exciting adventure. With guilt and fear gone, a whole new world of motives opens before us.

Well, my summer adventure in Pennsylvania was quite a learning experience. I returned in triumph to Columbia Union College, not realizing what would happen during my junior year.

Fateful Retreat

8

AFTER my lonely adventure in Pennsylvania, I could hardly wait to get together with friends for the new college year. And my brother Bill would be rooming with me. That past summer he had become a Christian, a thrilling answer to prayer.

On registration day I switched my major to theology, having decided to become a pastor. Several weeks previously I had preached my first sermon to a little congregation in Johnstown, Pennsylvania, and had savored the experience (more than my audience did, no doubt). Based on my evangelistic labors that summer, church leaders in Pennsylvania unofficially decided to hire me upon my graduation, an opportunity somewhat unique for a junior. They counseled me to start looking seriously for a life partner with whom to share my ministry.

There were plenty of nice candidates available, and I relished the opportunity to get to know them. Selling techniques learned in my summer work helped me line up dates. For example, in sales you never question whether prospects want your product. Of course they do! So you offer them their choice of cash or monthly payments. Likewise, a guy should assume that the girl he likes also wants to go out with him. So he confidently (without seeming arrogant) offers her a choice between Friday night vespers and Saturday night dinner. If she doesn't want either option, she can still say no.

Well, before long my weekends at college became a delightful blend of spiritual and social fellowship. And my daily theology classes offered insight and inspiration for future work as a pastor. Life was exciting. For the first time ever I felt on top of the world. The Good Shepherd had put me in green pastures.

My happy days lasted all of two months. Then suddenly I sank into a valley of despair and confusion deeper than anything I had ever suffered, even before becoming a Christian. My big plunge began the night of October 22, 1971. I was attending a student retreat in the hills of Maryland, hoping to enhance my joy in the Lord and service for Christ. The speaker that weekend was an elderly minister who headed a self-supporting institution. I noticed he seemed unusually somber as he rose to address the students. He announced that we would be studying the reason for the delay of Christ's second coming.

"Think of all the years gone by since we expected Jesus to return," he implored as his piercing eyes swept the audience. "Why has our Lord not yet come?"

I had often wondered about that in the year since becoming a believer. What *was* keeping Jesus from coming back?

"The answer," the speaker asserted with eyebrows raised, "is that Christ is waiting for every one of His people to live perfectly without sinning. We must overcome all sin before He can take us to heaven."

It was a daunting thought indeed, and mind you, he wasn't referring to sins of rebellion committed by unsaved people. He emphasized that the failure of genuine Christians to become perfectly sinless was preventing Christ from coming. He illustrated this point by comparing Jesus in heaven to a mother mopping the kitchen floor. She can't put down the mop until all her children quit tracking in mud. Likewise Jesus can't stop what He is doing in heaven and return to this earth until every Christian quits muddying up heaven's book of record by having sins to confess.

Could this possibly be true? I wondered. I could feel the joy of my life, my assurance of salvation, vaporizing in the cool night air. I squirmed in my seat as the speaker solemnly disclosed more bad news. "Every time we fail in our attempts to please God, we not only delay Christ's coming, but we bring crucifying pain to His loving heart. Jesus is like a railroad engineer pinned beneath the wreck of this world's sin, and our mistakes are like scalding water from a ruptured locomotive boiler dripping down upon Him. Not till every believer achieves absolute Christlikeness of character will the load be lifted from Jesus and His awful agony cease."

How terrible! I thought as a big lead ball formed in my stomach. *But if it's true I've got to believe it. I've got to accept it. What can I do to overcome all my sins so Jesus can stop hurting and I'll be fit for heaven?*

"The path to perfection," declared the speaker, "is spending much time in prayer, continually contemplating the terrible cost of our sins, which are breaking Christ's heart. Only then can we appreciate the value of Christ's life-changing sacrifice. Only then will we love Jesus enough to stop sinning forever. Only at that time can Jesus finally return to this earth for His perfected people."

All this appealed to my sensitive conscience. Not until years later did I learn that it's not the burden of guilt but the peace of God, the assurance of His acceptance, that keeps our hearts and minds in Christ Jesus. "The joy of the Lord is your strength" in overcoming temptation (Neh. 8:10).

Certainly it's true that only by understanding Calvary's cost can a stubborn sinner repent and come to Christ. But once we surrender our hearts to Jesus, it's time to flush away guilt and celebrate His acceptance. God wants His people to bask in the sunshine of His love.

A sense of divine disfavor brings discouragement, thus threatening emotional health. Not only that, spiritual paralysis results. Worst of all is the eternal loss that comes from refusing to entrust oneself to the Saviour's merits. The Bible warns those who hope to qualify themselves for heaven by their conformity to the law: "You have become estranged from Christ, you who attempt to be justified by law; you have fallen from grace" (Gal. 5:4, NKJV).

A solemn warning indeed!

Well, that night at the student retreat my agonized mind couldn't find sleep. I tossed and turned at the horror of my Lord suffering torment every time I missed an opportunity to witness for Him. Here I thought Jesus was happy with me during the past year since I had given my life to serve Him—only to find out now that I'd been torturing Him instead and delaying His coming.

By the time morning dawned, I made a firm covenant with God that by faith in Christ I would overcome all sin. I would develop the closest possible relationship with Jesus so that He could perfectly live His life in me. Then He could return to this earth in clouds of glory and take me home.

Sunday afternoon I returned to campus a changed person. My friends noticed it immediately. By midweek they were asking, "What's wrong, Marty? You seem kind of sad." I asked them to pray that the Lord would help me overcome all sin and help others experience that transformation also.

By the end of the week I had mimeographed a yellow sheet with the heading "How to Stop Sinning." It was crammed full of the depressing things I had learned at the retreat. I circulated that miserable paper all over campus—in the cafeteria, the dormitories, the gym, the chapel, everywhere. I confess I felt like a hypocrite telling everybody else how to stop sinning when I had not yet attained that lofty goal myself. Not because I wasn't trying, though. I rose earlier than ever in the morning to deepen my relationship with Christ and obtain His overcoming strength. But I ran into a big problem. The closer I came to Jesus, the more aware I was of my shortcomings—and the more guilty and despairing I felt.

This is unreal, I thought. *Getting close to Jesus only makes me feel more sinful and depressed by comparison to Him. What will it take to become exactly like Him so I can finally have peace?*

I stopped at nothing in my quest for a Christlike character. Seeking to quench all competitive pride, I quit playing sports. To close every door to potential temptation, I stopped dating. To keep my mind absolutely clear, I quit eating desserts. To avoid the danger of disease, I swore off dairy products. No more ice-cream cones. Now that was something of a sacrifice, but nothing compared with closing the little black book on my social life. At every step, I followed the Spartan blueprint advocated by that speaker from the self-supporting institution.

A year before, when I became a Christian, I had surrendered sin's dead leaves; now I was breaking off life's innocent branches. All I had left was a dying stump.

Despite my drastic efforts to achieve perfection through the strength of Christ, I couldn't deny that I was still a sinner. No big failures, you know. Just that general imperfection of fallen human nature in coming short of God's ideal.

"Why haven't I become perfect yet?" I lamented to one of

my friends who had roomed with me at that fateful retreat. He admonished me to search my heart again for some secret fault that must surely be obstructing the Holy Spirit.

But what did I have left to give Jesus that He didn't already have? The only thing I could think to do was to quit the Christian college that permitted its students the freedom to indulge themselves in strawberry shortcake and hot fudge sundaes.

So I bade farewell to my brother Bill and all my friends. Farewell to my scholarships. Farewell to my college diploma, my theology degree, and my cherished dream of becoming a pastor. I heard about a place far away in the hills of West Virginia that seemed conducive to sinlessness. It was a self-supporting community affiliated with the retreat speaker's institution. The people there believed as I did about perfecting Christlike character, and they kindly invited me to join their group.

I had a hard time locating where they lived. Finally I found the little dirt road that dead-ended at their property. *Such a pure, natural setting*, I thought as I hopped out of my car and surveyed the tidy gardens and simple, sturdy buildings. *Nothing here will distract me from pursuing my perfect relationship with Christ.*

Survival was a struggle out there. Mornings I would hand crank the old John Deere tractor and plow the fields. Or I helped fix the rust-encrusted vehicles we drove, sawed firewood, or built little houses for incoming families. All afternoon the year round I sold Christian books and magazines up and down country roads and hollows. Then every evening and all weekend long I conducted Bible studies in surrounding towns.

Life at the institution was anything but lavish. No television, no radio, no newspapers, no magazines, no suppers. No income except for a $20 monthly allowance to cover tooth-paste, postage, Bibles, and tapes. Not a dime did we "waste" on clothing—the women sewed dresses for themselves, some-times made from used bed sheets. Since I didn't sew, I satisfied myself with old-fashioned suits donated for the thrift shop.

Nothing I could rummage up would fit my lanky frame that required 38-inch sleeves. Even the longest suits didn't come within three inches of reaching my wrists. My pants failed to cover anything south of my lower shins. I looked like Bozo the Clown. No kidding.

But nobody cared how I looked. I didn't even care myself anymore. If anything, I was grateful that my humble appearance had delivered me from worldly pride. But then I became spiritually proud of my humility.

Some of the women and girls didn't bother shaving their legs. At first that struck me as rather crude, but then I thought, *What difference does it make?* Dating was illegal at our self-supporting institution. Of course, who would have wanted to go out with a Howdy Doody like me, except for some Raggedy Ann? If my friends from college had seen me, they would have had a good laugh. Or maybe they would have cried.

Leaders at our institution controlled the lives of their subjects, even the adult workers, by dispensing their "counsel." Their word was law. If they suspected that I might enjoy learning electrical work, for example, they typically assigned a different job, like cleaning the barn. All this, of course, was for the sake of developing character. It was as if I had joined a monastery and had taken vows of poverty, chastity, and obedience.

No problem, though. I willingly submitted to the discipline of my spiritual leaders. After all, they quoted inspired writings to support everything they did. Besides, all they wanted to do was help me attain perfection. Once perfected through Christ's power we could all go to heaven, and life's misery would be past. So I imagined.

Occasionally visitors interrupted the routine of institutional life. We knew they were coming by the cloud of dust moving up our road. Some of these visitors were quite wealthy and supported our institution with their gifts. They were impressed and even intimidated by our Mother Teresa lifestyle. The food we ate, the songs we sang, our plain manner of dress—everything seemed so simple and pure and holy. Our guests would write out a big check (tax-deductible) and promise to pray for our work. Then, satisfied that they had paid their debt to the poverty-equals-piety gospel, they drove off in their Mercedes.

Watching their cars escape to civilization, I couldn't help feeling proud of all I had given up for Jesus. But such humbler-than-thou smugness only left me with a deeper burden of guilt. Spiritual pride was the great sin of the Pharisees, I knew. Was I somehow backsliding spiritually—despite my ceaseless sacrificing?

One thing that alarmed me about myself was my growing hard-heartedness toward animals. I had always loved pets, especially cats. (As I write this chapter, my Siamese cat, Louie, is curled up on my lap.) But while attending the institution, I got to the point where I didn't want pets around. If a cat rubbed against my legs, I would ignore it or shove it aside with my foot. Pets were just useless distractions on my path to perfection.

You may think that I was quite a legalist, and yes, I certainly was. But believe it or not, I considered myself an apostle of righteousness by faith. You see, my motive in self-denial was to rid myself of anything that would deter me from depending upon Jesus and becoming like Him. My whole goal was to perfect a victorious faith relationship with Christ.

Christ-centered legalism, that's what it was. Instead of accepting Christ's accomplishments as my own, I competed with His righteousness. I failed to see that depending upon Christ means first of all accepting His perfect record as my own. Like Cain of Bible times, I was putting fruit on the altar of salvation—the fruit of the Spirit—rather than trusting the blood of the Lamb.

Certainly every true Christian will bear fruit for God. But when we start measuring our fruit to see whether we are worthy of heaven, we cease to trust Christ's blood for our salvation. Instead of accepting Christ's righteous record, we compete against it.

As with everything else, there are two opposing extremes in relating to the gospel. "Liberals" tend to downplay the importance of following Christ's example, indulging in a cheap praise-the-Lord gospel of presumption. "Conservatives" tend to downplay the need for trusting in Christ's blood, promoting a gospel of legalism. The truth is that we need both Christ's forgiveness and His example—we depend completely on His blood while we unreservedly obey His example. And since our sincere efforts always fall short of absolute likeness to Christ, our faith must remain firmly rooted in His mercy.

Sooner or later, legalism tends to bog down in so called

health "reform." That's because no matter what you give up for Jesus, you still have to eat something. So food becomes a big focus in character development, and health reform degenerates into health deform.

Some of us at the institution kept an eye on each other's food consumption, prepared to pounce upon any perceived shortcoming. At one breakfast I took a heaping tablespoon of peanut butter, and someone scolded me. She insisted that only a teaspoon of peanut butter was healthful. Anything more than that might clog up my stomach, thus drawing away blood from my brain that is needed to help me think clearly so I could keep my mind on Jesus.

Now as I look back on it, I can see how stupid and petty this nonsense was, but it was all in the name of Jesus, pursuing a faithful relationship with the Lord of our bodies. We were attempting to qualify ourselves for heaven through Christ's perfecting power rather than by finding our only refuge in His saving blood.

Please understand that I do believe in the importance of maintaining good health. But I don't think it should be the big focus of our gospel.

There's something else I must clarify here. I believe that independent ministries and self-supporting institutions have a vital role to play in finishing God's work. They certainly have a right—a responsibility, in fact—to urge fellow Adventists to quit compromising with the world. But tragically some of these groups, claiming to uphold the foundation of faith, actually wage war against the church organization that God ordained. Worse yet, they sometimes forfeit the gospel of grace and entrap unsuspecting souls in legalistic bondage.

I confess that I went to greater lengths in my legalism than anyone else at the institution. The leaders there called me a fanatic. I thought, *Great! Everybody calls these people fanatics, and now they're calling me a fanatic. That makes me the fanatic of the fanatics! Praise the Lord, I'll be a fool for Christ's sake! These folks here just aren't spiritual enough to relate to what God is doing in my life.*

Things got worse. I started imagining myself under the special inspiration of God. This "inspiration" involved the Lord "giving" me tunes for various Psalms as I read them. Every morning I came forth from my devotional time with some new melody that I'd proudly share with anyone who had the patience to listen. I guess I pictured myself as a modern-day David, the sweet singer of Israel. In retrospect, I realize that my songs weren't all that sweet. In fact, some of them were downright sour. If God ever "gave" me such tunes now, I'd be tempted to give them back!

My safari into musical composition was just a pitiful attempt to convince everybody that I had a unique baptism of the Holy Spirit. In reality, I couldn't even convince myself of that.

Everything came to a climax one Saturday night. I was in my little attic room meditating on Christ's invitation, "Come to Me, all you who labor and are heavy laden, and I will give you rest" (Matt. 11:28, NKJV). I got to thinking. *Rest—how sweet it sounds! If only I could enjoy real rest in Jesus.*

Suddenly something inside me exploded. *God, what does it take? I've already given up everything You could possibly want. I've given up sports and desserts. I've forfeited my scholarships and my hope of being a pastor. I've given up my family and all my friends, even the nice girls I was dating. I'm all alone here. My class at college is graduating this spring, and I'm stuck here on this old farm where nobody loves me, nobody cares.*

Hot tears cascaded on my Bible. *They call me a fanatic, Lord. But all I do is only what You want me to. I just study, work, and pray. And I sing those songs to You—and still it's not enough! I still feel guilty all day long!*

I convulsed with sobs, unable to control myself. *God, what do You want? What will it take for me to have that perfect Christlike character? Why can't You help me stop hurting Jesus and be ready to go to heaven!*

How long I spent sobbing on my knees, I don't know. When I finally got up, I was more determined than ever to overcome sin—even if it killed me. And kill myself I almost did.

Legalism by Faith

9

AFTER my sobbing subsided, I rose from my knees and vowed to redouble my efforts to stop sinning. Not in my own strength, of course, but in the power of the living Christ within me. Then I crawled onto my Army cot and dropped into an exhausted sleep.

The next day I fasted and prayed. I was already a frequent faster, but now I determined to deprive myself more often. Not to gain merit, you understand, but to clear my mind for a deeper relationship with Jesus. When others were feasting on physical food, I chose to feast by faith on the Bread of Life.

Thanksgiving Day of 1973 stands out in memory. We were to enjoy an abundant holiday dinner, which I considered a test of my spiritual commitment. While the others enjoyed their meal, I climbed the mountain behind the institution and fasted. I prayed for everyone by name that they would not overeat and defile their body temple.

I did my best to convince myself that I was having a better time fellowshipping with the Lord than if I had been indulging my appetite. The truth was that my growling stomach made me resent the others who could eat their meal without guilt. Ironically, my fasting left me worse off spiritually than if I had simply enjoyed Thanksgiving dinner like everyone else.

Obviously, fasting was not my pathway to perfection. What else could I do to make my Christian experience more productive in achieving sinlessness? I thought about my sleeping habits. The Bible warns against wasted slumber. I was sleeping only six or seven hours a night, but was even that too much? Should some of that time be invested in extra prayer to enhance my faith relationship with Jesus? My favorite books told me that Christ prayed all night, and His example in doing so was for us to follow. Our Lord was refreshed without sleep by communion with His Father, I read, and for us as well as for Him earnest prayer never wearies but always refreshes.

Well, I concluded, *that's it! If the Lord says I should pray all night, I'm going to do it.*

Thinking that Christ had no advantage over us of any kind, I believed that the same spiritual and physical strength He received through prayer would refresh me equally as well. And so I made my decision. Through Christ's power I would live the rest of my life without sleep. All things were possible through faith.

That night after returning from my Bible studies it was time to launch my new prayer life. I wrapped a blanket around me and flashlight in hand ventured outside. The chill November air seemed to pierce through my shivering frame as I toiled up the mountain. Arriving at my chosen place of prayer, I knelt on the freezing ground and poured out my heart to God amid the sound of the wind moaning through the trees. Not far away a bobcat screamed—or was it a mountain lion? I prayed on. The frost forming on the ground glistened in the moonlight as I agonized before my Maker.

Why was I praying outdoors? Because Jesus did, and I believed in following His example. By faith, of course. Everything I did was by "faith."

About midnight my frostbitten mind couldn't think of anything else to pray about. I rose stiffly from my knees and stretched my numb frame. Then I stumbled down the hill and back inside the house to study the books of Ellen White and my Bible. After an hour or so of reading, I warmed up enough to start nodding off to sleep. Catching myself just in time, I hurried down to the cellar to take a cold shower. Nothing in the world would rob me of this vital season of spiritual refreshing. Finally, about 3:00 that morning I did doze off, to be awakened a couple hours later by my buzzing alarm clock.

Night after night I maintained my lonely vigil. It was like a self-inflicted Siberian exile. Some freezing nights my resolve sagged, and I returned to the house early, telling the Lord I would study the rest of the night—only to slip off to sleep about midnight. I can hardly describe the guilt I felt upon awakening after "wasting" five hours of sleep. I condemned myself for betraying my Lord, missing out on essential fellowship with Him.

Often I did manage to pray and study the whole night through. Yawning triumphantly, I would set my books aside, rub my weary eyes, and join the rest of the institution for morning worship. Somehow I found the strength to face a full day of hard labor.

I kept a careful record of my sleepless hours to measure my spiritual growth. To this day I have my notebook with those records.

People at the institution tried to help me. They would show me counsels written to students about getting proper sleep.

"That's good counsel for students who haven't attained full maturity as Christians," I replied. "But look here—in the *Testimonies* it says Christ prayed all night, and His example in doing so is for us. Do you believe that?"

They couldn't think of what to say, so I seized the offensive. "You can compromise if you want to, but I'm not going to explain away inspired counsel to suit human weakness. All things are possible through faith!"

"You're losing your mind," they warned.

"No, I'm not losing my mind. I'm finding my Lord in a deeper way."

Then I quickly found a statement about Christ's brothers charging Him with losing His sanity because He prayed so long and worked so hard. "Jesus did exactly what I'm doing," I chided them. "And like Christ's unconverted brothers, you're trying to stop me!"

What could they say? I pressed the point, accusing the workers at the institution of compromising their own convictions. They often criticized church members who didn't take inspired counsel literally—yet they themselves were watering down these clear statements about Christ's example for us in sleepless prayer.

In all my fanaticism I was simply taking the principles they claimed to believe to their logical conclusion. They often expressed guilt about not praying enough. Well, I *was* praying enough. They confessed that they weren't studying the Bible enough. I *was* studying enough. All I was doing was what they seemed to feel guilty about not doing. Nevertheless, they called me a legalist.

"No!" I protested. "I'm only doing this to deepen my relationship with Jesus."

Yet of course what I was doing was legalism—Christ-centered legalism. I pictured myself staying awake all night with my Lord. Everyone else was asleep, like the faithless disciples slumbering in the garden of prayer.

You guessed it—that old demon of spiritual pride had overtaken me again. I was a real pain to live with. Although I secretly hated myself for being self-righteous, I still couldn't stop feeling smug. There was no denying the fact that I lived on a different spiritual level than anyone around me.

Why couldn't everyone see that sleeplessness is the secret of perfection? It seemed so simple—God has two ways of refreshing us: through sleep and through prayer. Carnal Christians were sleeping away precious hours of spiritual refreshing, praying just enough to love the Lord but not enough to experience His total victory. But I was drawing from the well of continual spiritual refreshment, quite literally praying without ceasing. At the end of time, I imagined there would be 144,000 perfect saints hiding in the mountains and praying all the time. And I would be one of them. Maybe even the first one of them.

Number one for Jesus. Why not?

Legalism, you say. Yes indeed, legalism at its worst. But remember it was Christ-centered legalism—legalism by faith.

Recently I've been fascinated by the history of the medieval church. I was startled, even shocked, to discover that everything I used to do, the recluses in their monasteries did during the Dark Ages.

I forsook family and friends; so did they. I denied myself marriage; so did they. I lived in poverty; so did they. I obeyed my superiors; so did they. I fasted; so did they. I maintained sleepless vigils, and so did they. And I did it all for the same purpose as they did—to attain a perfect union with Christ by faith.

Consider the Roman Catholic devotional classic *The Imitation of Christ*. Written by a German monk in 1427, a full century before Luther's Reformation, this medieval manual on legalism by faith advocates the same lifestyle I used to follow. "St. Lawrence, through the love of God, overcame mightily the love of the world and of himself. He despised all that was pleasant and delectable in the world. . . . Instead of man's comfort he chose to follow the will of God. Do in like manner, and learn to forsake some necessary and some well-beloved friend for the love of God" (p. 87).

You see, it was to get close to God that devout monks and nuns abandoned their friends and families. They were pursuing the same purifying relationship with Christ that I was. "My son, says our Saviour Christ, I must be the end of all your works, if you desire to be happy and blessed. If you refer all goodness to Me, from whom all goodness comes, then all your inward affections will be purified and made clean" (*ibid.*, p. 118).

Did you know that the medieval church believed this way about Jesus? "Offer yourself to Me and give yourself all for God, and your oblation [offering] will be acceptable. . . . But if you have trust in yourself and do not freely offer yourself to My will, your oblation is not pleasing and there will not be between us a perfect union" (*ibid.*, p. 218).

A perfect union with Jesus was the cherished goal of the medieval monks. Their obsession with perfection through a relationship with Jesus is a trademark of ancient and modern Catholic writings.

Martin Luther thundered against this Christ-centered legalism by faith, but he had to learn the hard way, as I did. After spending much time in the monastery in search of perfection, he finally accepted the perfect record of Jesus Christ as his own accomplishment. Back when he had entered the monastery, he had determined to become holy. He pursued purity by depriving himself of life's comforts, even its necessities. Some nights, kneeling on the cold, stone floor, he would console his conscience, "I have done nothing wrong today." Then doubts would arise. "Am I really pure enough to qualify as a child of God?"

Nothing he could do brought him peace. He could never be certain of satisfying God. But finally he discovered that the peace he was trying so hard to obtain was waiting for him at Calvary's cross. Jesus took the punishment that we sinners deserve, so we could be freely forgiven.

Luther could hardly believe this good news. Despite his guilt he could be counted as perfect, since Jesus, who really was holy, suffered his penalty.

Of course, the Catholic Church had always taught that only through the power of Christ can sinners be saved. However, Luther came up with a challenging new discovery: Believers, although imperfect, can at the same time be counted righteous. God considers sinners to be saints as soon as they trust in Jesus—even before their lives reveal good works (which of course will be forthcoming).

Notice Romans 4:5: "To him who does not work but believes on Him who justifies the ungodly, his faith is accounted for righteousness" (NKJV). So the ungodly who surrender to Jesus are justified, forgiven. Forgiveness comes not because we are holy. Not by works, Luther now realized, but because sinners trust in Jesus.

All his life Luther had thought it would be unfair to reward imperfect people with eternal life. He believed in purgatory, a place where after death imperfections could be purged to make Christians fit for heaven. But now he learned that "all have sinned and fall short of the glory of God" (Rom. 3:23, NKJV). Even the saints fall short of God's perfect ideal. Our only hope is the blood of Jesus Christ.

Luther came to realize that because Christ is our substitute, every Christian is already worthy for heaven. On the cross Jesus "qualified us to be partakers of the inheritance of the saints" (Col. 1:12, NKJV). There is no need for purgatory! Joy filled Luther's heart. Finally his troubled conscience found peace through the gospel and he escaped monastic bondage.

Like Martin Luther, I had to leave my "monastery" before I found peace. But before I did, my quest for perfection almost killed me. Let me explain. After having just a couple hours of sleep—or no sleep at all—I almost killed myself driving to my Bible studies. Time after time I fell asleep at the wheel, only to wake up just in time to avoid a head-on collision. Often I jolted awake just as my wheels hit the gravel shoulder of the road, about to plunge over the embankment into the river.

Yes, my sleepless legalism almost killed me. But honestly, I wouldn't have cared. What did I have to live for? I never considered suicide—I wouldn't dare take my life into my own hands after committing it to God. It would have been fine with me, though, if God had ended my life. I think I secretly hoped that would happen.

After all the wretched things I suffered in my younger years, the Lord had restored my soul and led me into green pasture —only to have the devil plunge me into this valley of death. And remember, Satan did not entrap me through the allurements of the world but through my sincere desire to obey God.

Can you see why, for the sincere Christian, legalism is a far more dangerous deception than worldliness? Every honest heart knows it's wrong to play around with sin. Legalism, however, appeals not to the love of sin but to our love of God and desire to obey Him. It robs our spiritual life by hijacking our purest motives.

I hate legalism! In the name of Christ I'll fight it till the day I cast my unworthy crown at His feet. Well, it took quite an act of God's providence to save me from my deadly bondage to legalism. Let me tell you how He did it.

First the Lord got me away from that self-supporting institution. I had planned to stay there the rest of my life, but in March of 1974 the president of the Mountain View Conference of the Seventh-day Adventist Church offered me a job as a pastor. He had no idea how legalistic I had become. All he knew was that in early 1972, shortly before I joined the self-supporting institution, I had led a task force of college students on a temporary assignment in literature evangelism.

That project had gone well—we got a church started in the Ohio River valley town of Point Pleasant. Based upon that success, the president wondered if I would serve as a part-time pastor in the mining village of Rainelle. The Adventists had a little white church building there that had closed down several years earlier. My job was to start up another congregation there. They couldn't afford to pay me a regular salary, but I could supplement my stipend of $40 a month by selling *The Bible Story*. Hopefully I could build up the church enough to become a full-time pastor.

Here was a chance to resurrect my dream of becoming a pastor. I would have to enter the ministry through the back door, without a college diploma, but God could use me anyway.

Taking up the challenge, I rented an abandoned shack on top of a mountain for $10 a month. It had no electricity and no running water, so I had to bathe out of a bucket by the well. The cows who grazed up there didn't seem to mind my presence. And I didn't mind parking my car by the highway and hiking three miles up the wooded trail to my hillbilly hideaway.

I plunged myself into my ministry, preaching the only gospel I knew—the same old legalism, and very few responded. The only lady I was able to baptize became so emotionally ill she had to be put in the state hospital shortly after I finished my studies with her. The poor woman already had problems before I met her, but I certainly didn't help her much.

Word reached the conference president about my warped teaching and weird lifestyle. One morning a letter arrived from him. In tactful terms he warned that my "spiritual growth" needed to be "much in evidence" before November when my progress would be reviewed. The implication was clear—my fledgling ministry was on the verge of oblivion.

Diamond in the Rough

10

THAT letter of dire warning from my conference president came as quite a crushing blow. Now, looking back, I understand. Something had to be done to harness my demented legalism.

Actually, I had been making some headway spiritually. For one thing I had started allowing myself some sleep again—I found it impossible to maintain a ministry living like a night owl. And I even was eating—with a clear conscience—some groceries from the store. Progress was slow but sure, yet there was not enough of it to win the confidence of the conference president.

Thank God that before probation closed on my ministry a new leader arrived, Tom Mostert. He introduced Steve Gifford as his director of ministers. Steve adopted me as his special project, convinced that I was some kind of diamond in the rough. He scheduled a visit to Rainelle to salvage my ministry. Would you believe it, though, I thought the Lord was sending Steve down to learn from me! My legalistic arrogance was exceeded only by my ignorance.

Steve's obviously a sincere man, I thought. *Confused but sincere. Maybe I can teach him something about true Christian standards.* You see, Steve wore suits that he had purchased from a store rather than my style of thrift-store rejects. Not only that, he drove a new Datsun B-210. I felt he ought to be humble enough to drive an old beat-up clunker like I did. Worst of all, Steve had a bad habit of eating a little supper, while I always fasted. If Steve ever hoped to receive God's seal of full approval, he had to quit compromising and abide by the standards. *Steve will learn,* I told myself. *He loves the Lord enough to change.*

I invited him to conduct a week of revival meetings in the Rainelle community fire hall. He gladly agreed to come and asked me to reserve a room for him in the local motel.

What a waste of the Lord's money, I thought, *spending*

$14 a night for a motel room! There was another place on the far side of town called the King Koal Hotel. The absentee owner kept it only as a tax write-off. The King Koal was rather run-down, to be sure, but rooms cost only $5 a night. Five dollars was still a lot to pay—whenever I traveled I preferred to sleep in abandoned buildings, if I couldn't stay in a private home.

When getting a church started in Point Pleasant, for example, I recall hitchhiking to town and finding an abandoned house across from a graveyard. Carrying my flashlight, I sneaked inside, brushed aside rat droppings on the couch, and went to sleep. Before dawn I slipped outside unnoticed and walked down to the Laundromat to wash in the sink and freshen up for another day of soul-winning.

If I could sacrifice like that for the Lord, certainly Steve Gifford could too.

I'll get Steve straightened out, I assured myself. *We can pray together, and his heart will be touched.*

Well, on the appointed day I met Steve at the post office, and we set off for the good old King Koal. Upon arriving there, he seemed hesitant to get out of the car.

"Is this where I'm supposed to stay?" he asked incredulously.

"Sure is!" I chirped. "What do you think of it?"

Steve didn't answer. He only sat there staring in amazement at the building. And what a sight it was! Its rusty neon sign hung from one hinge. Roof tiles were missing. The weather-beaten clapboard siding apparently hadn't seen paint since World War II. It definitely was not what you'd call a five-star resort. It was the pits.

After finally emerging from the car, Steve and I ventured up the creaky front steps. He looked like a soldier tiptoeing through a mine field. We passed through the shattered glass door and entered a lobby that looked like something out of Edgar Allen Poe. It was dark and spooky, with only one 40-watt bulb casting shadows behind the metal desk.

As we stepped up to the counter, the elderly hunchbacked clerk set aside his dog-eared porno magazine to wait on us. Service with a smile it wasn't. We paid our $5.00 in cash—American Express cards were not accepted, for whatever reason.

Having successfully checked in, we mounted the creaking steps to Steve's room. And what a room it was! When I plunked down the suitcase on the lumpy bed, a cloud of dust soared into the stale air. Cockroaches paraded across the threadbare brown carpet. The bedside lamp didn't work. The toilet, however, did work. It worked too well, in fact, flushing even when you didn't press the handle. I'm exaggerating, but not much.

Steve didn't say anything. He just bit his lip and held his peace. The next morning when I came by to go out visiting with him, the poor man was scratching from bedbug bites. He suggested that we have a little chat.

"Marty, have you ever read in the Bible about the laborer being worthy of his hire? Don't you think my work for the Lord qualifies me to enjoy a $14-a-night room? Besides, what do you think the respectable people of this community will think of our church when they hear about me staying in this shack? Marty, you ought to reconsider your concept of Christian standards, don't you think?"

I had to admit that Steve was right. Even so, I wasn't ready as yet to surrender my sacrificial lifestyle. Several days later Steve and I were sitting in his little Datsun, studying the map, when he took a deep breath and straightened up. "Marty," he said solemnly, "look at me. I don't know if I've been getting through to you or not. But do you know how close you are to losing your ministry because of your legalistic attitude?"

Well, that got my attention. For the first time since leaving college I allowed myself to question the wisdom of my suffocating scruples. That night while going to sleep I mused, *Maybe I'm the one who needs to get straightened out.* The next morning during my prayer time I finally concluded: *Steve's right! I've been a foolish fanatic. How could I have been so blind?*

A tidal wave of shame swept across me. Here I was running around in my stupid Bozo outfits while Steve dressed like a respectable man of God. His shiny Datsun not only looked better than my rusted lowrider, but it also ran reliably. While I was crawling in the mud to reattach my muffler for the umpteenth time, he was sitting in somebody's living room leading souls to Christ.

It was Steve's soul-winning influence that really opened my eyes. People loved to be around him, whereas my somber scruples repelled them. Steve radiated God's joy, but I exuded nothing but misery. Steve's life revealed the fruit of the Holy Spirit, whereas I was a barren thornbush of legalism.

This painful contrast between Steve's character and mine humbled me in the dust. No, God didn't send me to teach Steve; He sent Steve to teach me. And at last I was ready to learn. So was my wife.

Happy Day

11

IT'S ABOUT time that I introduced you to Darlene, my wife. We got acquainted at the self-supporting institution I've been telling you about. She first caught my attention because of her sympathetic heart and refreshing honesty. She seemed unpolluted by hypocrisy. She also loved to go from house to house offering Bible study guides. Between the two of us we actually conducted more Bible studies than the rest of the institution put together.

We didn't work side by side, you understand. The institution forbade an unmarried man and woman to drive to town together or spend any time in each other's private company. The only loophole in that policy involved washing dishes. You could talk together all you wanted while scrubbing pots and pans. So the kitchen sink soon became the social hot spot of the institution.

As the weeks went by, I found myself drawn to Darlene, and decided I wanted to marry her. I asked the Lord to help me get approval for initiating a "courtship" (the nineteenth-century term used for dating). You see, before initiating any discussion of a possible relationship between prospective partners, the man had to get permission from the institution's leaders and also the parents of the young woman. Believe it or not, even before an adult woman worker could accompany a man to a health food picnic, he was supposed to clear it with her parents (if they were still alive)—after he got the green light from the institution.

No doubt about it, launching a courtship was no easy task. First the institution leaders determined whether the would-be suitor was suited for marriage. Then they evaluated whether the woman of his choice was indeed the one he ought to marry. Ideally, he would ask them to suggest a wife for him. If he already had someone in mind, they usually withheld or delayed approval.

Absolute authority lay in the hands of the institution's leadership. Questioning their wisdom was regarded as rebellion against God. Maybe that has changed now; I don't know. I'm just relating what happened to me.

Since I already had my heart set on Darlene, my chances of getting permission for our courtship were not good. But maybe God would work it out, I hoped. I prayed for the proper opportunity to present my request.

I saw my chance when one of the leaders of the institution was giving me a haircut. Since we were outside the house on the front porch, I felt sure the conversation couldn't be overheard by others above the whine of the electric clippers. I chose my words carefully: "I'm into my 20s now, and I've been thinking about a life partner. I like Darlene a lot. May I have your permission to begin a courtship with her?"

Seconds ticked by while he pondered my request. My fate was in his hands. I hardly dared to breathe. Finally he frowned and shook his head. "I'm sorry, Marty. You're not ready to get married. For one thing, with all your fanaticism you're not spiritually mature. And what about your finances—how could you ever hope to support a wife?" He also expressed doubts about whether Darlene and I were suited for each other. He concluded by emphasizing how important it was for me to obey his counsel.

That was it. The door was shut. Months of dreams and prayers were smothered in a three-minute conversation with a man who controlled my life.

My heart sank as I started the tractor and headed off to plow the field. For three days I could hardly eat anything—my stomach seemed awash in acid. I've never experienced such abdominal pain before or since.

Whatever my disappointment, there was some wisdom in discouraging me from pursuing a relationship with Darlene. I was indeed entrapped in fanaticism (although I didn't realize it at the time) and so in no way suited for marriage. As for my finances, my situation was undeniably hopeless. But what chance did I have of improving my condition when they paid me only $20 a month? Especially since they forbade workers to earn outside income! So how could I *ever* get married?

Not everyone at the institution was as poor as I was. Even though we all received the same monthly allowance, both of the leaders had been wage earners in the real world before joining the institution. So they already had their furniture, a late model car, and some money in the bank. But I came to the institution with nothing but religious books and an old car bound for the junkyard. Under such unjust circumstances, it seemed unfair for the institution's leaders to sit in judgment on my finances.

What perplexed me most about having my courtship denied was the directive that I "obey counsel." Obey counsel? Only a command can be obeyed—counsel is just advice. Counsel left me free to weigh the pros and cons and make my own decision.

I determined to get some genuine counsel from respected Christian leaders outside the self-supporting system. None of them expressed concern about my interest in Darlene. When I mentioned this to the leaders of the institution, they declared that all such counsel was invalid. They asserted that nobody but self-supporting workers really understands Christian standards.

Well, the institution sank my love boat, but the Lord had His own plans for my relationship with Darlene. Even though I was forbidden to discuss the matter with her—and I strictly obeyed the rules—she seemed to sense my feelings. I had no idea how much she really did know. You see, through the providence of God she had listened to every word of the conversation during my haircut.

Here's how that came about. The afternoon of my haircut she happened to stop by her room at just the right moment to catch an unexpected earful. Through her open window, above the din of the electric clippers, she heard me mention her name. Curious, she paused to listen to what I was saying. She was surprised—up to that time she had no idea I even liked her. As it turned out, she herself already liked me.

As the summer wore on, we often found ourselves at the kitchen sink, discussing topics of an approved nature. For example, we lamented the worldliness in the church and praised the importance of prayer. Often we exchanged a favorite text or some inspired quotation—all for the sake of fostering faith, you understand. But I noticed by the look in her eyes that she had come to care a lot for me. Somehow the language of love transcends words and cannot be easily repressed.

Winter came and went, and the mountain wildflowers began to bloom. For a whole year I had been talking to no one but God about my feelings for Darlene. Now I went back to the institution's leaders and asked if they thought my situation had changed. They replied, "No." According to them, I was still immature spiritually and insecure financially. They again warned me to obey their counsel and forever abandon any hope of marrying Darlene.

At this point I found myself questioning the wisdom and methods of the institution's leaders. They meant well, certainly, but who had set them up as counselors above God's ordained church leaders? Where did they get the authority to control the personal lives of adults nearly their own age?

About this time the conference president called me to work in Rainelle. I had mixed emotions about leaving the institution with Darlene still working there, but duty called.

As I packed my suitcase, one of the leaders came in and informed me that the institution felt it necessary to impose a total blackout on me. No contact with Darlene was allowed—no phone calls, no letters, no visits. Out of regard for Darlene, who still had to live there, I agreed to abide by their decision.

Just before I left, my work supervisor came to my room and bluntly informed me that I would never make a success of my life. He said I was marked for failure—just the encouragement every earnest young worker for the Lord needs to hear!

Years later I met that man again, during a weeklong series of revival meetings that I was conducting for an appreciative audience of several thousand. One night I spotted him in the crowd, the very man who had assured me I'd never amount to anything. I made it a point after the meeting to search him out. He seemed a bit sheepish, reluctant to look me in the eye. I guess he was surprised to see me doing something useful after all.

The day I left the institution, driving down the dirt road for the last time, I didn't feel very useful. Not to the Lord, or to Darlene, or anyone else. The loneliest summer of my life awaited me. For months I didn't see Darlene or talk with her—except to glance at her from across the aisle in the auditorium at camp meeting.

During the communication blackout that summer, people at the institution tried their best to persuade Darlene to forget about me. Their plan backfired, however. Their high-handed tactics in smothering our relationship opened her eyes. She began to question the claims of such self-supporting institutions to represent true Christian principles. Who gave these leaders the right to exercise absolute control over another adult's personal life? Darlene also grew weary of hearing my character defamed. She loved me—and nothing they said or did could change that.

Knowing nothing of what was going on, toward the beginning of August I contacted the head of the institution and once again asked his permission to talk with Darlene. By this time he was getting tired of keeping us away from each other. He unexpectedly agreed to let events run their course.

"All right," he said, "you can have your courtship. But since you have disobeyed our counsel, God cannot bless your relationship. And we think it might be best under the circumstances if Darlene left the institution."

Happy day! I acted swiftly to take Darlene and move her away, finding her an apartment in Rainelle where I worked. But her decision to leave did not come easy. She felt like a nun abandoning her convent. Dire warnings about life in the outside world under my influence left her full of fear. Yet somehow, convinced that the Lord was leading us, she found courage to cast her lot with me. Within two months we were married.

That was in October 1974. The following January, Steve Gifford joined our conference as director of ministers. I invited him to share lunch with Darlene and me in our one-room garage apartment. Everything went smoothly enough until he asked to use the bathroom. You see, we had no bathroom. He could take his pick between the night pot and the outhouse. He chose the outhouse.

That was a new experience for Steve. I can still see him picking his way through the weeds and gingerly shutting the outhouse door behind him.

Bless his heart, Steve had faith that sooner or later we would break the shackles of our legalism. I don't know anyone who would have put up with as much fanatic nonsense as he did in trying to help us. And his efforts paid off.

To begin with, Darlene and I got ourselves some real clothes. I had a sharp new navy blue suit tailored for my long arms—how good it felt to discard my Howdy Doody duds and wear something respectable again. Darlene struggled violently with her conscience about changing her wardrobe. Back at the institution, a little old lady had convinced her that modesty required Christian women to uphold nineteenth-century fashion standards. Pauline Mostert, wife of the conference president, took up the challenge. In her gentle but direct way she counseled Darlene to wear something decent instead of those ankle-length dresses, something appropriate for the time in which we live. Darlene accepted her good advice, but she still felt terribly guilty that first morning in church, wearing a knee-length dress. Gradually that false guilt faded away, along with all the bad memories of our past.

We had a new life now, with new clothes and some new furniture. All this involved expense, of course. Again it was Steve Gifford who came to the rescue, arranging a supplement to our poverty-level paycheck. With this we moved out of our hillbilly headquarters and rented a little house. We even put a down payment on a new car, something we desperately needed.

You see, one day on my way to a ministers' meeting the fuel pump on my old blue junker took an unscheduled sabbatical. Every 15 minutes I had to pour cold water on it to coax it back to work. Driving along a mountain road beside a river, I had access to all the cold water I needed. No problem there, but alas, I didn't have anything with which to carry the water back to the car. Finally, in answer to prayer, I located some discarded beer bottles and put them to better use than they had known before.

Well, by that time I was running late. Afraid my tardiness wouldn't make a good impression on my ministerial peers, I hurriedly cast the empty bottles behind my seat and hit the road. I made it to the meeting on time, but . . . later that day I noticed some of the men clustered around my car, peering inside at my beer bottles. I had some fancy explaining to do, believe me.

(Never afterward have they let me forget it.) After that narrow escape, I thought I'd better get a loan and buy another car before I found myself out of a job.

Owning a new car was important to me. That Dodge Colt didn't cost much even by 1976 standards, only $3,300. But its purchase was a rite of passage on the road of respectability away from my junkyard lifestyle. It also helped me keep my appointments—no more breakdowns and beer bottles.

This rebirth in our lifestyle reflected our spiritual rejuvenation. The understanding that legalistic poverty does not equal piety set us free from making ridiculous and destructive sacrifices. Nothing we bought was lavish by any means. All of it merely helped us serve the Lord efficiently without bringing reproach upon our profession.

Tom Mostert via Steve Gifford kept close tabs on our progress. He spent time with us too, helping immeasurably. I remember when he drove down to visit me. We sat in my office and opened our Bibles. He patiently explained that the word *perfection* actually means "maturity"—a consistent Christian life of uncompromised commitment. It has nothing whatever to do with attaining an absolutely sinless character. Our only hope is in the blood of Christ. Certainly every true believer will cooperate wholeheartedly with God in overcoming sin, but our salvation is not measured by our spiritual successes.

Thank God for the good news from Tom Mostert that our ticket to heaven is not our perfect sinlessness, but the mercy of God through Jesus Christ. My confidence in salvation sparked a growth spurt in the two churches under my care. Attendance increased dramatically as my members welcomed liberation from legalism. New converts swelled the ranks. I think I led the conference in baptisms, even as a part-time pastor.

With such evidence of God's blessing upon my ministry, the conference leaders welcomed me into full-time employment. Words can't describe the thrill I felt when the envelope bearing my pastoral credentials arrived in the mail. I held up that little white card to the Lord and praised Him with all my heart for salvaging my ministry. Five years before, when leaving college, I forfeited all hope of ever becoming a pastor. Now, incredibly, that dream was being fulfilled.

Along with my full salary, the conference added a third church to my district. By this time Darlene and I were expecting an addition of our own. So it was that little Stephen Thomas came into this world, whom we named in honor of the two men who served as Moses in delivering us from the bondage of legalism and bringing us into the promised land of ministry.

I'll never forget the day our son was born. Early the morning of May 27, 1976, Darlene shook me awake with excitement sparkling in her eyes. "I think today's our day!" We grabbed the prepacked suitcase, jumped in our new Colt, and raced the 35 miles to Greenbrier Valley Hospital.

"Slow down," Darlene admonished. "We'll get there in plenty of time."

"You mind the baby while I mind the road," I retorted as we careened around another mountain curve. It was a good thing we hurried. The blessed event occurred mere minutes after we screeched to a halt at the hospital.

Words can't describe what I felt when I saw baby Stevie for the first time. My own son! The little fellow taught me instantly what no adult could have taught me in a lifetime. Through him I learned how our heavenly Father feels about His children. I longed to protect my child from all harm and pain. So does God. I loved the little guy even though I knew he'd dirty his diapers—just as God loves us even though He knows we mess up. I didn't expect absolute perfection from my son, just warmhearted loyalty in response to my love—exactly what God wants from us.

Baby Stevie grew up to be daddy's boy. When he was 14 months old Darlene went to the hospital to give birth to his sister. With her away for three days, my son slept on my chest, heart to heart with Daddy. When Mommy came home with little Christiane Angela, she laid her in the crib and sat down with Stevie to cuddle him. Nothing doing. He jumped off her lap and toddled right back over to me. I didn't mind that at all, you understand.

Steve and Christi, now teenagers, are still the joy of our lives. We play ball together, chase the cats around the house, and hike to the beach. Now and then we take a weekend off together and drive up the coast.

For Darlene and me, the last remaining scars of our past are being healed. It hasn't always been easy, with the incredible adjustments we've had to make in our lifestyle and our faith. But love for God, our children, and each other has united our lives and brought us happiness.

Calm Before a Storm

12

ONE Sunday morning I was romping with the kids in our living room when the phone rang. It was the new conference president. "Marty, listen. We have a special job we want you to do. Would you consider serving as our conference evangelist? You would be traveling around the state holding meetings in various cities. We're sure the Lord would bless you."

What a challenge, on top of all the other changes happening so quickly! In 1976 I had become a full-time minister. The next year we transferred to the church in Huntington, one of the larger cities in our conference. In October of 1978 I was officially ordained to the gospel ministry. Now our new conference president was calling me to be an evangelist.

It didn't seem possible that a mere four years ago Steve Gifford and I had had our little chat in the King Koal Hotel. Since that time both he and Tom Mostert had moved on to larger responsibilities, but their labors and prayers on my behalf had established me in the Lord's work. And now I had this new opportunity! The best part of my work would be training younger pastors in soul winning while holding meetings in their districts. I might even be able to rescue some King Koal fanatic, just as Steve helped me. It all seemed like a dream.

As always, Darlene was eager to take up a new challenge with me. We decided that the whole family would travel together from meeting to meeting, an arrangement made easier because our kids were still preschoolers. The conference helped us buy a big used trailer, two slide projectors, and some sound equipment. Then I had to prepare a complete series of evangelistic sermons.

At last all things were ready. In February of 1979 we left our house in Huntington to go forth and win converts to Christ and His truth. My first crusade was scheduled for the village of

Parsons, West Virginia. The town itself was rather drab, but massive mountains, towering evergreens, and pristine rivers adorned the surrounding countryside. Unfortunately, not many residents were around to enjoy the scenery. No doubt the conference leaders selected an area of sparse population for my first meeting so I could cut my evangelistic teeth without causing too much damage.

My personal expectations were sky-high, though. We rented the community hall above the fire station and mailed brochures advertising my Revelation lectures. Everything was set to go. "If we can only have good weather," Darlene remarked, "I believe we'll have some great meetings."

February was indeed a risky time to launch a crusade in the mountains of West Virginia. Sure enough, the day before opening night we had a heavy snowstorm—nice for the ski business but not so good for us. And when the snow finally stopped falling, the temperature fell. Then our trailer pipes froze. So did my fingers when I crawled around in the snow trying to restore the running water.

Somehow despite it all, the meetings got off to a good start. Perhaps two dozen visitors attended, along with our handful of faithful church members in Parsons. On the front row night by night sat two families with open Bibles on their laps. Even the children marked every text. Such enthusiastic Christians were just the people I needed to spark new life in our dying little church.

Everything progressed smoothly until I presented the seventh-day Sabbath. Suddenly both families disappeared, leaving the front row depressingly empty. The next morning I hopped in my car and raced over to their neighborhood to persuade them to come back.

With a prayer in my heart and the Bible in my hand, I knocked on the door. The lady who usually spoke for the others welcomed me inside, but with something less than her usual smile. "We missed you the last couple nights!" I exclaimed. (In other words, Where were you people?) She was happy to explain. "You know, preacher, when we first heard about your Sabbath, we thought we might have to leave our Sundaykeeping church. But yesterday our pastor showed us in the Bible that we're not under the law. So we don't have to keep the Ten Commandments—including the Sabbath!"

"Well, would you mind sharing with me what texts he showed you?" I challenged.

"Sure. Let's find Romans 7." While turning there, I told myself, *We'll get this nonsense straightened out right away!*

She asked me to read verses 4 and 6: "Therefore, my brethren, you also were made to die to the Law through the body of Christ, that you might be joined to another, to Him who was raised from the dead, that we might bear fruit for God.' "
" 'But now we have been released from the Law, having died to that by which we were bound, so that we serve in newness of the Spirit and not in oldness of the letter' " (NASB).

"There you have it, Preacher!" she declared. " 'We died to the law.' 'We've been released from the law!' It's right there in the Bible!"

"But that's talking about the ceremonial law," I protested.

"No," she chided me. "Look at the very next verse. What law do you see in verse 7?"

" 'Thou shalt not covet,' " I read.

"And where do we find that commandment?" she inquired triumphantly.

I gulped and admitted that the passage must be discussing the Ten Commandments after all. I tried to quickly divert her attention to James, but nothing doing. In two minutes I was slinking out the door like a beaten dog.

Those families never came back to the meetings, as you might have guessed. But we did baptize five precious souls.

After the meetings finished, I could hardly wait to get home so I could open my concordance and solve the mystery of Romans 7. Before my next crusade opened in Oakland, Maryland, I had to get to the bottom of what Paul meant about being dead to the law through Christ.

I discovered the key to Romans 7 a few verses earlier, in chapter 6:14: "For sin shall not be master over you, for you are not under law, but under grace" (NASB). Here was the crucial question that would answer everything: What does it mean to be under grace instead of under the law?

That lady in Parsons thought grace provided her a blank

check to do as she pleased, transgressing the law. Actually, the verse indicates just the opposite: "Sin [breaking the law] shall not be master over you." Grace provides power over sin "in order that the requirement of the Law might be fulfilled in us, who do not walk according to the flesh, but according to the Spirit" (Rom. 8:4, NASB).

Now that's ironic, I thought. *Living under grace provides power to keep the law, but living under the law—that is, a legalistic, law-centered life—robs us of that power. Why is that so?*

I knew there is nothing wrong with the law itself, of course. But something happens when the law points out our guilt: "Sin, taking opportunity through the commandment, produced in me coveting of every kind; for apart from the Law sin is dead" (Rom. 7:8, NASB).

Amazing. Somehow our sinful nature takes advantage of the commandment "Do not covet," to produce the very behavior forbidden. And this despite our earnest commitment to obey God's holy law! Paul even declared that sin has no power apart from the law. How could this be?

Well, the law makes us feel guilty, which worsens our spiritual situation—all the guilt in the world can't help us stop sinning. Guilt breeds discouragement, that famous tool of the devil. We feel paralyzed with despair from resisting further attacks of temptation. That drives us deeper than ever in sin.

Now we see why so many sincere people succumb spiritually. The law condemns them, leaving them guilty and depressed. *What's the use, anyway?* they wonder. And they plunge deeper into sin—all because of the condemnation of the law. No wonder the Bible concludes that "the power of sin is the law" (1 Cor. 15:56, NASB).

I had seen a dramatic illustration of this startling truth in the life of a man whose funeral I conducted. He had been a deeply committed Christian soul winner. Even in retirement he won many converts throughout the conference. Everyone spoke well of that gentle man, yet he obviously carried a burden of some kind. Nobody knew just what it was that troubled him.

They found out one cold and gray morning when he shouldered his shotgun and told his wife he was going outside to shoot a rat. Then he kissed her goodbye for the last time. Moments later she heard the shot that ended the life of that wonderful Christian man.

His funeral was one of the saddest I've ever conducted. The unspoken question seemed to be on everybody's mind: What caused such a godly man to kill himself? What caused him to pull the trigger?

The answer came that afternoon. Following the service I was sitting with the widow on her front porch swing as she showed me his book of sermon notes and his diary. It was quickly obvious what had killed this good brother. Guilt had shot him.

Shot by guilt! Here was a man who had no problem opening the New Testament and proving the importance of keeping the law. But when it came to overcoming personal sin, his diary revealed a wrenching story of nagging failure. No big sins—just enough to discourage him with the continual evidence that he fell short of Christ's example in fulfilling the law. He agonized, "Here I've been telling everyone else to keep the law and I can't even keep it myself. What hope do I have of heaven? Why go on?"

But was the law itself to blame for killing this poor man? No, the commandments are "holy, righteous and good" (Rom. 7:12, NASB). They only told him right from wrong. But in doing so, the law exposed his sinfulness so efficiently and vigorously that he became hopeless and desperate, failing worse than ever. All because of guilt! Finally the guilt got so bad it murdered him.

The lesson was clear. Any attempts to qualify ourselves for salvation by measuring up to the law will yield the fruit of failure. "The sinful passions, which were aroused by the Law, were at work in the members of our body to bear fruit for death" (Rom. 7:5, NASB).

It's a vicious cycle. The law condemns our guilt and leaves us discouraged, driving us deeper into sin. And the deeper we fall into sin, the louder the law condemns us—which makes us sin even more.

How nice it would be to get rid of guilt by fleeing from the condemnation of the law! And thank God, such an escape is possible. We can be fully and freely forgiven in the compassionate arms of our Lord Jesus Christ. His perfect life and death fulfilled all righteousness on our behalf, meeting every demand of the law for our salvation. This is the good news of the gospel.

A heart set free by God's free grace is the secret of personal power. As Paul the apostle said: "Now may the God of hope fill you with all joy and peace in believing, that you may abound in hope by the power of the Holy Spirit" (Rom. 15:13, NKJV). "The joy of the Lord is your strength" (Neh. 8:10).

Wonderful news, you may be thinking. *But surely saving grace doesn't release us from spiritual responsibility.*

Not at all. The Bible says we "died to the law through the body of Christ . . . that we might bear fruit to God" (Rom. 7:4, NIV). This fruit for God through the freedom of forgiveness replaces spiritual failure, that "fruit for death" from the old life of guilt.

So living under grace provides power to obey God: "We have been released from the law so that we *serve* in the new way of the Spirit, and not in the old way of the written code" (Rom. 7:6, NIV). This word *serve* in Paul's day literally meant "to slave." You wouldn't expect a slave to run around town doing as he pleased. He must obey his master's will. So with the Christian—we serve Jesus. We live according to His will, not ours.

That night it was raining when I drove home from the funeral. As my windshield wipers squeaked back and forth across the glass, I reflected on my old life of legalism. Just like the man I had buried, my faith had been crushed under the load of the law's weighty demands. But now under grace I was free from the burden of perfectionism to serve the Lord without fretting about my shortcomings of character. The new atmosphere of acceptance and assurance sparked within me a spiritual growth spurt. With guilt gone, my heart responded in gratitude and love for God—and the joy of the Lord provided power to honor those same commandments that used to be so oppressive.

Living under grace has also brought me a new dimension in keeping the Sabbath. During my dark ages of legalism, I considered the Sabbath some kind of 24-hour tightrope upon which to perform before God and demonstrate how holy I could be—through the power of Christ, of course. In other words, I went to Mount Sinai to keep the Sabbath, just as the ancient

Pharisees did. Now on Sabbaths I go to Calvary.

At the cross we see the true meaning of Sabbath rest. As Jesus died for our sins, He cried, "It is finished!" His mission was accomplished. Mankind was redeemed! Then, as the sun began to set for Sabbath, the friends of Jesus laid Him to rest inside the tomb, where He remained over the Sabbath hours to memorialize His completed work on our behalf. Now when we rest on the Sabbath, we show our acceptance of His accomplishment on Calvary as our salvation.

The law demands a finished work from us: "Six days shalt thou labour and do all thy work." Yet when the sun goes down each Friday afternoon, we look around at all the things left to do. We must confess that our work isn't done by any means. Nevertheless, God invites us to lay aside our unfinished business and rest in the work Christ completed for us.

So Jesus earned the right for us to enjoy Sabbath rest. Do you get the picture? There's tremendous therapy for legalism in the Sabbath. Many who want to please God wind up trusting in their own works for salvation. I used to be among them, rummaging around in my life's record, looking for evidence that qualified me for heaven. Now, week by week the Sabbath assures me that despite my shortcomings I stand complete in Christ. The Sabbath keeps me clinging to the cross for God's amazing grace.

Keep in mind that living under grace doesn't mean dishonoring God's law. Grace brings power to truly keep the commandments. Of course, we still fall short of God's glorious ideal—but no sincere believer need worry about failures. "There is therefore now no condemnation for those who are in Christ Jesus" (Rom. 8:1, NASB).

Can you imagine how our homes, our schools, and our churches will be transformed when we cherish God's mercy as our only hope of salvation? With our hearts secure in His acceptance, we'll have convincing power to share that good news.

I'll say this—preaching this gospel of grace in a deeper way certainly enhanced my evangelism. Conversions in my meetings multiplied as people responded. In one small city, for example, we baptized 27—more than had joined our church there in quite a while.

As the year 1979 came to a close, I was riding the crest of success as never before in my life. I couldn't imagine how things could get better.

It was only the calm before a storm.

Trouble With Truth

13

I T WAS Christmas season, 1979. I had just concluded my first season as conference evangelist. Having survived it with a measure of success, this should have been a time of special celebration for me. Instead, I found myself in trouble. Nothing financial, moral, or family-related. The problem centered on my understanding of the judgment.

Seventh-day Adventists have always believed that in the year 1844 in heaven Jesus began a new phase of His high priestly ministry for His people—a judgment of those who claim to be believers to see if God can take them to heaven.

Ever since my childhood I fervently believed in this judgment in heaven preceding Christ's coming. I have to confess, though, that my convictions failed to bring me peace of mind. In fact, traditional Adventist teaching about the judgment was an unceasing source of spiritual insecurity for me.

"Until we overcome all sin," our pastors often warned us, "we are not prepared to meet the Lord in peace. Even now the books of judgment are open in heaven. Even now that solemn judgment may have passed to the names of the living. Mercy lingers, but not for long. May God give us grace to let Jesus live out His perfect life within our hearts."

All this I believed as strongly as anyone else. But now I discovered that my understanding of the gospel clashed with my belief in the judgment. Doubts swirled in my mind, such as: Why would God jeopardize the security of believers by subjecting us to a judgment? And what is the purpose of judgment, since God already knows those who are His?

These questions had begun bothering me the previous summer. It all started at a workers' retreat at Valley Vista, the picturesque campground of the Mountain View Conference. I took advantage of the opportunity there to lay plans with the pastors for whom I would be holding meetings. I also wanted to get close to them so that we could work well together. Several of them had a Bible study going, which I joined upon their invitation.

On the patio walkway that surrounded the lodge we opened our Bibles and entered into discussion. I soon discovered that these fellows had some fundamental doubts about Adventist doctrine, especially the pre-Advent judgment. They contended that such theology is not only legalistic but also nonbiblical, resting instead on the writings of Ellen G. White.

I tried to help them, but instead became confused myself. Soon my mind boiled over with questions—questions I wanted to dismiss. Why not just warn these guys that they are into heresy and tell them I don't want to study with them anymore? Why risk being identified as a dissident?

You see, the pastors were already under suspicion, having disclosed their doubts to the conference president. But unlike Tom Mostert before him, our new leader seemed unable to relate well to some of the younger workers. Instead of being able to sit down with them and discuss their questions in a nonthreatening manner, he admonished them with a father's strong authority. He warned them that they were out of harmony with the Bible and the inspired counsel of Ellen White—and they had better get back on track.

I had little to gain and much to lose by plunging into such a debate over doctrine. Our president appreciated my work and believed in me—he had just installed me on the conference executive committee. After years of floundering around in anonymous fanaticism, I was on the fast track to really big responsibilities.

On top of this, I loved my work preaching Adventist doctrine —and it fed my family. The last thing in the world I wanted was to get myself in trouble with the president of our conference.

No, not quite. The last thing I wanted was to disobey God. How could I become a time-serving politician—a hypocrite?

What's more, I had always told my evangelistic audiences that there is only one reason to belong to a church: all its teachings must be found in the Bible. "If your church is out of harmony with the Word of God," I admonished, "leave it and join a body of believers that does teach the truth—the Seventh-day Adventist Church family."

That challenge worked well for me during my year in evangelism, bringing people into the baptistry. Now I had to take my own medicine. If it turned out that the Adventist Church was not in harmony with the Bible, then I would have to resign my ministry and leave the church I loved. That was the only way I knew to be honest both to God and to my conscience. Besides, I couldn't just walk away from those young workers who were all friends of mine. They needed my help. What real danger could there be? We Adventists are fond of reminding fellow Christians that truth has nothing to hide from the Bible. So why should I hide?

I made my decision. I would follow wherever the Lord led me in His Word. I would ignore the risks and keep studying with the pastors.

Never before did I enjoy such brotherhood as I did with those three guys. Before our monthly workers' meetings, we would rent a motel room, where we'd search the Scriptures together till the morning hours. But our joy did not last. I soon received a phone call from the president.

"Marty, I would prefer that you stop studying with those pastors. You fellows are out of the mainstream in your thinking and are headed for nothing but trouble."

I agreed to comply with his directive. Then I asked him if he had considered the possibility that something might be wrong with the mainstream of church thinking, since we had expected the Lord to come for so many years and still He has not come. I frankly confessed to having serious doubts myself about Adventist doctrine and told him that my conscience required a definite biblical base for belief. Even if the church disagreed with my conclusions.

At this point the president was thoroughly alarmed. He arranged for the ministerial director to take me to the Ellen G. White Estate to regain my doctrinal moorings. I was touched by the kindness that met me there, but remained convicted to resign unless I could somehow find evidence that our Adventist doctrine of the pre-Advent judgment is taught in Scripture and is fully in harmony with the biblical gospel.

My intentions were sincere enough, but looking back now, I believe that our little "gospel" group had developed a "we versus they" mentality that had traces of arrogance. Perhaps if we had humbly worked to bridge the widening gap between ourselves and the president, we might have won unity and mutual tolerance. Despite our sincerity, our failure to do this was inexcusable. By God's grace I finally recovered and survived, but my friends eventually resigned or were removed from the Adventist ministry.

Now I was the only one of our study group left in the church. Night after night the questions that drove them away nearly drove me out of my mind. How ironic—throughout the conference, people I had baptized were rejoicing in the church, and I who had led them there was writhing in the valley of decision. For the first time since my self-supporting days I started getting depressed.

My mind needed to know: If Adventists teach the truth about God's Word, somebody please help me answer from the Bible this terrible challenge to our beliefs. I wished I could simply brush aside these questions, as so many others seemed able to do.

But I knew I had to keep studying. What I finally learned made me delighted to be a Seventh-day Adventist and greatly increased my assurance in Christ.

The key to my new understanding was the ancient Hebrew meaning of judgment, which is quite different from our own legal system. You see, our society requires judges and juries to be strictly neutral. If they harbor a bias either in favor of or against the accused, our law demands that they disqualify themselves. Not so in Bible times. Back then the legal code required judges to abandon neutrality and take the side of the defendant. The defense of the accused was a duty so sacred that the judge refused to delegate it to a defense attorney. Instead, he himself served as the defender of the accused.

The *Jewish Encyclopedia* explains that "attorneys at law are unknown in Jewish law" (Vol. II, p. 293). Their legal code required judges to lean "always to the side of the defendant and [give] him the advantage of every possible doubt" (W. M. Chandler, *The Trial of Jesus*, vol. 1, pp. 153, 154).

Witnesses of the crime pressed charges, while the judge promoted the case of the defendant, biased in favor of acquittal. (See Taylor Bunch, *Behold the Man!* pp. 77-79.) Now we understand why David in the Psalms longed to be sentenced by divine judgment: "Judge me, O Lord my God, according to thy righteousness; and do not let them rejoice over me" (Ps. 35:24). Throughout the Old Testament God's people found joy in His judgment: "A father of the fatherless, and a judge of the widows, is God in his holy habitation" (Ps. 68:5). Of course, the judge also had to execute justice. If evidence of guilt could not be controverted, he had to abandon reluctantly his defense of the accused and pronounce condemnation. But the whole Old Testament system was predisposed toward vindication, not condemnation.

I was beginning to see light at the end of the tunnel for my future in the Adventist Church. I thought, *If only our people understood the biblical meaning of judgment, they would realize that God is on our side, defending our salvation. What a difference it would make for their peace of mind!*

What I had learned was already beginning to make a difference in my appreciation for Adventist teaching. Important questions remained, though. If God is defending us in the heavenly judgment, who would dare withstand Him?

In studying further I saw that it's the devil who raises questions about our salvation in the judgment. The Bible calls him the "accuser of our brethren," who accuses us "before our God day and night" (Rev. 12:10). Apparently Satan is jealous about our going to heaven, where he used to live when he was Lucifer, prince of the angels. And so he accuses God's children of being unfit to pass through the pearly gates.

Well, we are unworthy, aren't we? How do we counter his accusations? Notice Revelation 12:11: "And they overcame him because of the blood of the Lamb" (NASB). Only through the blood of Jesus can we overcome the devil's accusations. God can't deny Satan's contention that we are sinful. But in the blood shed on Calvary's cross He finds the evidence He needs to pronounce us innocent. So He dismisses Satan's charges, endorsing the security in Christ we have enjoyed since we accepted Him.

Now, in certain situations the Hebrew judge appointed an advocate to assist him in defending the accused. The *Jewish Encyclopedia* states that the husband could represent his wife and help the judge defend her if the verdict involved his personal rights (Vol. II, p. 294).

Here we have a thrilling parallel with the heavenly judgment. Christ, bridegroom of the church, purchased us with His precious blood. Now He serves as our court-appointed advocate to help the Father defend us from Satan—and to defend His own right to take us up to heaven and share His home forever. It's wonderful news! God in the judgment takes our side against Satan. Jesus our advocate assists Him by interceding for us. God finds in the sacrifice of His Son the legal basis to accept repenting sinners and count us perfect.

I like that, don't you? It made me feel confident in Christ about my salvation! And it has also done wonders for my wife. As you might imagine, Darlene was quite confused at first by all my questions. She hardly knew what to think. But through it all she stayed by my side, joining me in my quest for truth. Together we welcomed every ray of light God sent our way.

One day we saw an illustration of our new understanding of the judgment—while shopping at the supermarket, of all places. I was standing in line with Darlene, leaning on our grocery cart. The kids found themselves utterly fascinated by the candy rack and hoped to persuade us to let them have an unscheduled treat. First they tried Milky Way bars. Nothing doing. Then M&M's. ("These have peanuts, and peanuts are good for you, Daddy, aren't they?") When that failed they reached for the last resort, sugarless chewing gum. You parents know what I'm talking about.

Anyway, this was going on when a wonderful realization suddenly struck me. Here we were, waiting so confidently in the checkout line without any doubts that the groceries were going to be ours—this despite the fact that there was a judgment of sorts to pass before we could take the goods home.

The clerk had to decide if we were "worthy" of having the groceries. And what was it that qualified us? It was the money we had in our hands. With cash to present the clerk, the groceries would unquestionably be ours to take home.

Heaven's judgment is something like that. Jesus is the treasure we need to pass the celestial checkout. With Jesus we can be assured of a favorable verdict, whatever our sincere struggles may be. God isn't threatened by our faults and failures. Just as the Safeway supermarket decided beforehand that whoever has money qualifies for groceries, God has declared that everyone who is in Christ qualifies for heaven.

Can you see it? The test of the judgment is not whether we are worthy in ourselves. The question is whether we have faith in Christ.

I'm not promoting some cheap, second-rate gospel that permits all kinds of monkey business under the guise of faith. True Bible faith requires commitment—commitment to Christ that exchanges what the world offers for what He offers.

Well, I was thrilled with what the Lord revealed to me about the judgment as I waited in the supermarket checkout line. He gave me a much better treat than my kids were hoping to get.

But I still had the question: Why even have a judgment if God already knows who believers are? Obviously it isn't for the sake of informing God of something He doesn't know—so it must be to enlighten His creation.

Here I needed to consider the background of that great controversy between good and evil. Satan, father of lies, long ago raised doubts about God's fairness and integrity. He repeated these same charges during Christ's days on earth: "This man receiveth sinners!" In other words: "How can the Holy One accept those who are unholy? And if He can forgive sinners, why could He cast me and my angels out of heaven, yet build mansions there for fallen humanity?"

God can't brush aside the devil's accusations because His government operates through the loving trust and loyalty of the universe. So He must settle doubts about His trustworthiness. The Bible reveals that God will allow Himself to be audited: "Let God be found true, though every man be found a liar, as it is written, 'That Thou mightest be justified in Thy words, and mightest prevail when Thou art judged' " (Rom. 3:4, NKJV).

I discovered one more thing about the investigative judgment. Sometimes people feel bad about having their sins recorded in the sanctuary. But actually, as long as we remain in

Christ our sins are forgiven—guilt is gone! So it's not a record of our sins that God is keeping up there—it's the record of His forgiveness, His mercy in our lives.

The Lord doesn't dispute Satan's contention that we have sinned. But in the blood shed on Calvary's cross He finds the evidence He needs to pronounce us innocent.

The Judge is on our side! What a message we have for a fearful, lonely world.

I realize that in the few pages of this chapter we've only touched on my discoveries about the judgment. If you want to probe deeper, I suggest you read my book *Some Call It Heresy*, available from the publisher of this book. The 16 chapters in that book discuss in depth the questions I had back in 1979, and the answers that have kept me in the Adventist Church.

I can't find words to express my joy at having discovered the good news that heaven's judgment is a favor, not a threat to me as a Christian. And what a relief to be able to remain a Seventh-day Adventist with my conscience intact!

Having survived the crisis, I felt a need for a fresh start, a new field of labor where I could forget the past and get on with my ministry. That's when the call came for us to move to California.

Escape to California

14

I COULD hardly believe it! Tom Mostert, now president of the Southeastern California Conference, wanted me to move west and pastor the Anaheim church. What a joy it would be to work with him again!

So it was that in March of 1980 Darlene and I put our West Virginia house up for sale, loaded the kids in our VW Rabbit, and headed for California. That trip was one of the happiest weeks of our lives. We stayed in motels and enjoyed the stark and astounding scenery of the great American West.

As we drove along, we discussed what it would be like to lead a church in California. We'd heard that there was a lot of worldliness and compromising out there so we wondered if we would fit in. Tom assured us that there were a surprising number of conservatives as well, along with solid and dependable moderates. Since we would be working with a couple of highly qualified associate pastors to assist my ministry, we looked forward to a rewarding experience.

Our kids' main goal, of course, was to see Disneyland. I told them that I was going to be Mickey Mouse's pastor. They were getting too old to fool, but we enjoyed the little joke just the same.

Upon arriving in California, we rented a house in Yorba Linda, hometown of Former President Richard Nixon. It wasn't a fancy house by any means, yet the rent was twice what our mortgage had been in West Virginia. Had we wanted to buy a house, it would have been much more expensive yet.

My ministry got off to a booming start. Within six months attendance had nearly doubled, and baptisms were coming right along. Then I made a well-intentioned move that nevertheless turned into a major mistake and cost me dearly.

I had heard that most associate pastors feel unfulfilled in their role, suffocated by the senior pastor. I didn't want that to happen with my staff, so I decided to divide my authority equally among the three of us. We took a spiritual gifts inventory to determine where our interests lay, and then divided up responsibilities accordingly.

My strength was in soul winning, so I changed my title to pastor of church growth. My older associate had gifts in administration and counseling, so he became pastor of church life. The youngest on our staff had a heart for those who are hurting, so he became pastor of special ministries for missing members and hospital visitation. We also split the sermon assignments among us.

Since I didn't need the big corner office for my soul-winning visitation, I offered it to the pastor of church life. He could use it for counseling and subcommittee meetings. The deacons renovated a storage room for my new office.

Where was my mistake? I failed to consult with the conference president about dividing my responsibilities. He would have explained that it's virtually impossible for a staff to function without a designated leader. Every team needs a captain, and the conference had chosen me for that role.

It was fine for me to share some of my authority, but I didn't realize that many members would misinterpret such generosity as weakness. Suddenly I realized that people didn't seem to respect me as they once did, especially when I moved out of my office. It didn't seem very professional to them. They didn't want the man hired to be their senior pastor working out of a storage room.

I made the same type of mistake Jimmy Carter did as president. You may recall he started carrying his own luggage, trying to be a servant leader. In doing so, he somehow squandered the respect of our nation and foreign leaders, too. They wanted someone with a sense of the dignity of his office.

Of course, meek and lowly Jesus traveled the dusty roads of Palestine, and people didn't appreciate their Messiah acting like that. Judas in particular was offended. It's confusing, isn't it? I still don't know what is the right balance between servant leadership and maintaining the necessary trappings of authority.

My problems in Anaheim were further compounded because my pastor of church life was not a good choice for the responsibilities I gave him. As a student at California State University before his conversion, he had majored in political science, and he delighted in employing ruthless tactics in his ministry. After a while I became disgusted with his political ploys, convinced that the church was suffering because of them.

Of particular alarm to me was that this man had some fundamental doubts about Adventist doctrine, which he managed to hide from me at first. Then I noticed how he became irritated when in my sermons I stressed the importance of obedience to God's standards of holy living. I'm no legalist, but I believe that faith in Christ demands total commitment, and I preach that with all my heart.

I concluded that this man was on a road of his own that sooner or later would lead him outside our church. (My fears proved accurate—he renounced his Adventist membership and joined a different denomination.) If I didn't take decided action, I knew he would lead many of our members astray. So I announced to the staff that I would reassert my responsibilities as senior pastor of the church.

That didn't go over very well, naturally. My associate continually worked behind the scenes, undermining the goals I wanted to accomplish. And when he realized he would not get his way around the church anymore, he requested that the conference move him to a different district. Quite honestly, I was relieved to see him go.

But the damage was done. I was never able to provide the leadership that congregation needed. Now, looking back, I see how I erred, and how to do better in the future. Nevertheless, there's no question that I function better as a thought leader than as a people leader. And that's OK. I'm happy with the talents God gave me.

After several years of frustration in Anaheim, I decided that my ministerial skills were better suited for speaking and writing than in pastoring churches. I knew that in order to pursue such a specialty I had to complete my education.

Unfortunately, my conference had no provision for sponsoring me at the seminary, since I already was ordained. So, in counsel with Tom Mostert, I left Anaheim in early 1983 with the goal of supporting myself at Andrews University Seminary.

First I had to complete my undergraduate degree. Twelve years had gone by since I had left Columbia Union College, so resuming my studies was no easy undertaking. The solution for me was the adult degree program of Atlantic Union College. Every six months I flew to Boston for a week or two of intensive study and consultations, then I worked on my assignments at home, keeping in contact with my teachers. Through this fine program I did eventually graduate.

While completing my college work, I also wrote the book *Some Call It Heresy*, which I mentioned in the previous chapter. I mailed the unpublished manuscript to various conferences and found myself invited to speak at numerous camp meetings.

Every year since 1983 I've traveled around the United States and Canada as a camp meeting speaker. Nothing I've ever done has been more fulfilling and enjoyable. I love conducting seminars and revival meetings—and thanks to my Compaq laptop computer, I can do the writing part of my work between meetings.

At the Oklahoma camp meeting in July of 1983, I met Harold Richards of the Voice of Prophecy. He read a copy of my manuscript and liked it enough to ask me to work for him as director of ministry growth.

Two of the best years of my life I spent at the Voice of Prophecy. Then one afternoon in 1985 I was called to walk across the media center campus and meet with George Vandeman. He explained that the lady who for years had helped him write telecast scripts was seriously ill, and he wondered if I would consider a call to work for him at It Is Written. I was delighted!

Even so, it wasn't easy leaving the Voice of Prophecy, but I just couldn't turn down the opportunity to help prepare telecast scripts. For several months of transition I worked for both Harold Richards and George Vandeman, and then in September of 1985 I began full-time work as director of prayer ministries for It Is Written. I've also been chipping away on my master's degree in journalism at California State University in Northridge.

Thanks to some book royalties that God sent my way, I've been able to do something for my mother that she never expected. You see, ever since the family split up, she has struggled financially. Part of this is because she has always been so generous with friends and family members who need help—she has the heart of a philanthropist but the wallet of a pauper.

Mom was forced to retire early for medical reasons, and that worsened her financial situation. Her problems climaxed one night as she drove home from church in her old car. It stalled in traffic. She had to limp around in the rain trying to get it taken off the road and to a service station, where greedy mechanics gouged her.

When Darlene and I heard about her awful experience, we decided to take action. I called an auto dealership where Mom lives in Hagerstown, Maryland, and arranged a deal over the phone for a new Dodge Colt. Using my royalties as a down payment, I arranged a loan with my credit union. Then, unbeknownst to Mom, I flew to Washington, D.C., rented a car, and drove to Hagerstown.

To make sure she would be home, I arranged for her good friend Millie Hillebert to meet her for lunch. Instead, my brother Fred and I showed up at her door.

She thought I was home in California, of course, so you should have seen the look of shock on her face when she saw me. But that was only the beginning. We took her out for lunch at Wendy's salad bar. Then, on the way back to her apartment, we just happened to stop by the Dodge dealership and park next to a beautiful blue four-door sedan.

"How do you like that car, Mom? It's all yours!" Well, delighted isn't the word for how Mom felt about her car. She tells me that whenever she gets lonely, she goes down and sits in her car. It has the license plate "GR8-MOM." And she is a great mom.

I don't mind telling you what God helped me do for my mother in the hope that some of you might be inspired to pull a pleasant surprise on your own mother. It doesn't have to be a new car, you know. Maybe just some flowers. The sad day will come when you pick up the phone to call your mother and she won't be there. Anything nice we want to do we must do now.

I have always dreaded the day that I will have to attend my mother's funeral. Suddenly in August of 1989 it seemed like she might soon be attending mine.

Attack From Marfan

15

THE LOS ANGELES OLYMPICS was a gold medal experience for America. We were so proud of our athletes. Nobody sparked our respect more than Flo Hyman, captain of our women's volleyball team. Soon after the Olympics, though, a tragedy ended her life. She died of Marfan's syndrome,* the same mysterious disease the doctors said might kill me.

Following Flo Hyman's all-star performance in the 1984 Summer Olympics, she played professional volleyball in Japan. During one of the games she sprinted off the court for a breather and took her place on the bench. Suddenly she slumped over—dead. The coroner thought she had a heart attack. But Flo had been so healthy, and her arteries were clear of cholesterol buildup. It just didn't make sense. Her heartbroken family brought her back home and arranged for an autopsy. Only then did the truth come out.

Often the first diagnosis of Marfan's syndrome comes from the coroner. My diagnosis came in August of 1989 at Cedars-Sinai Medical Center in Los Angeles. Solemn-faced physicians summoned my family into a small white room and seated us in a circle of chairs. A licensed grief counselor sat next to my wife, keeping an eye on her as the doctor in charge addressed me. His voice was crisp and professional, yet soft with compassion.

"Mr. Weber, we're sorry to bring you bad news. We've concluded our consultation and have diagnosed you with

---

*Marfan's syndrome is named after the French pediatrician Anton Marfan, who discovered it back in 1896. In the century since then, medical researchers have learned that the disease results from an abnormal gene mutation at conception—but they haven't been able to isolate and identify that gene. Researchers feel they may be nearing a breakthrough, but there is still no simple genetic test available for diagnosis.

The National Marfan Foundation is a nonprofit organization dedicated to solving the dilemma of this disease and assisting its 30,000 sufferers in North America. Research and services depend upon donations. The foundation will be happy to answer any questions and refer suspected patients to qualified specialists. You can write to the NMF at 382 Main St., Port Washington, New York 11050.

Marfan's syndrome. You probably know this is a potentially fatal disease. We'll put you on beta-blocker medication to extend your life, but sooner or later open-heart surgery is anticipated to replace your aortic valve. You should understand, however, that despite all we can do for you, Marfan's often claims its victims unexpectedly, and fatality is immediate."

Darlene interrupted, "Are you sure Marty has this disease?"

"No question about it."

"But he's always been so healthy!"

"Being in good shape has nothing to do with it. Marfan's syndrome afflicts otherwise healthy people."

"But how does this Marfan's thing kill people?"

The doctor pointed to a chart: "The problem involves this big artery coming up from the heart, the aorta. Marfan's syndrome makes it balloon out like a big bubble, and then it suddenly bursts. Death, of course, follows immediately."

Darlene looked puzzled. "But why does that happen?"

The doctor explained further. "Marfan's syndrome degenerates the walls of the aorta until that bubble, or aneurysm, forms in the weakest area of the artery. It grows larger and larger, eventually stretching the wall of the aorta to the point where it ruptures. Although this death takes place without warning, the fatal aneurysm actually develops gradually, taking months and even years. The patient seldom realizes what's happening inside his chest."

The kids and I sat there silently as my wife asked her questions. Everything seemed so factual yet so bizarre. Was it really me they were talking about?

Darlene kept demanding answers. "Don't you doctors have some type of test to see if the aorta is about to burst?"

"Yes, we do. With an echocardiogram—an ultrasound picture of the heart—we can actually measure the aorta quite accurately. And when it begins to swell past a certain point, heart surgeons perform a life-saving operation. What they do is insert a Dacron tube into the aorta, which reinforces its walls. At the base is an artificial valve to replace the aortic valve."

While Darlene digested that information, I jumped in to ask, "What's it like living with Marfan's syndrome as you get older?"

"I'll be frank with you," the doctor said. "There's a lot of pain involved, both physical and emotional. Marfan's attacks your connective tissue in many places and in many ways. Your bones and joints, your eyes, your heart and blood vessels, the lungs —all will deteriorate. The most visible manifestation is something you already have: excessively long limbs in relation to the rest of the body—a wingspan even wider than your height."

"Well, I've got long arms, that's for sure. How long do most Marfan's people get to live?"

"Men with Marfan's have a normal life expectancy of about 40 years."

"That's great," I interjected. "I'll be 38 in a couple months."

"Let me finish," the doctor chided. "We can probably keep you around much longer—as long as you cooperate with us. You must get your echocardiogram tests and take your medicine."

"About those beta blockers," I said. "I don't even like taking aspirin. What are the side effects?"

"You'll no doubt lose some of your energy and feel somewhat sluggish. You might become impotent. Other things too. I'll give you a booklet to read about it. Now, even with this medication, you've got to keep your heartbeat down to reduce the risk to your circulatory system. That means no more mowing the lawn or hoeing the garden—for the rest of your life. And I hate to tell you, no more sports, either."

"No more basketball with my son?"

"I'm sorry, but no. No baseball, either. No running at all."

Thirteen-year-old Steve turned and looked out the window, watching the traffic on La Cienega Boulevard five stories below us. The poor guy was fighting back tears. Ever since he was a baby we had played together every day. No more now. It seemed that he had already lost his dad even before I died.

I tried a little gallows humor to lighten the atmosphere. "Well, I guess Steve and I can take up knitting."

"You can walk together around the neighborhood," the doctor suggested hopefully.

At this Steve could remain quiet no longer. "Only old people go out walking!" he retorted, still facing the window.

"There's one fun thing you and your dad can do. You can ride bicycles together—just as long as his heartbeat stays below 120. If his heart races above that, it will shorten his life."

Well, you can imagine how the family felt as we took the elevator down to the parking garage and headed home in our Camry. Even though none of us had much of an appetite, we dropped in at a restaurant. It was there that 12-year-old Christi broke down. She didn't care who heard her cry. She was going to lose her father.

That night after Darlene finally fell asleep, I slipped out to the living room to sit in my favorite blue armchair and talk with the Lord. "It seems to me that we've had a good thing going," I told Him. "Have You brought me through all the trouble of my life just to put me in an early grave? Or at least to spend the rest of my days as a semi-invalid?"

During nine years as a pastor I had visited numerous members with terminal illnesses or handicaps. Now it was my turn to suffer. Would all the spiritual gems I shared so easily then strengthen my own heart now? Or would anger and self-pity overwhelm me?

For a long time I sat in the darkness and pondered my life.

Everything was quiet except for the clock on the wall, which gently ticked away the seconds. Every swing of the unseen pendulum dragged me closer to my death. Yet God was good. He had exchanged my tortured conscience for a peace that knows no guilt or fear. And He blessed my service for Him more than anyone dreamed possible. It's a long way from that old sleepless farm of doom, where nobody wanted me, to the exciting nationwide ministry I now enjoy. So if, after all He had done for me, God wanted to take me out of this world, that was His business.

"I'm in Your hands, Lord," I told Him. "So do whatever You want. I've got just a couple requests. Would You watch over my family, especially Steve and Christi—be their Father after I'm gone? And please don't let this work You've given me to do stop happening. One more thing, Lord. During whatever time I have left, don't let me feel sorry for myself about being disadvantaged or handicapped."

Having settled all this with God, I turned on the table lamp and got my computer out of the briefcase. I typed out a letter for Darlene, to be held for her by my secretary until after my death. In it I thanked her for our many years together and encouraged her to carry on without me.

Then I wrote a letter for Steve and also for Christi to read after my death. "I'm so proud of you," I told them each. "Please don't blame God for what happened to me. Just stay faithful to Jesus so we can all meet again in heaven."

I don't mind telling you that those letters were not easy to write. I cried so hard that the cats ran out of the room.

After finishing those letters to my family, I made a list of 10 ministers and church leaders—people I respect but who don't seem to share the burden for the gospel that means so much to me. "Lord, if You will turn the lights on for these people and empower them with Your Spirit, You can take me out of this world—no questions asked. Just save my family and help me finish that book I'm going to write [this one you are reading]."

It might strike you as strange that I accepted my situation so quickly, without going through the normal time-consuming grief process. Actually, the bad news didn't come all that suddenly. A year earlier, after experiencing chest pains, I had had an echocardiogram that indicated MVP—mitral valve prolapse. Although many people have such heart murmur dysfunctions, in my case because of my particular body style it raised questions about Marfan's syndrome. The cardiologist at the time told me not to worry about it, so I didn't. But in September of 1989 I was scheduled for an overseas writing assignment that would involve strenuous mountain climbing. I thought I'd better get checked out for Marfan's syndrome beforehand. That's when I set up the appointment at Cedars-Sinai, one of the top four centers in the nation for diagnosing and treating Marfan's patients. So you see, when the bad news was confirmed that August afternoon, I already had had a year to prepare myself.

The next morning I went to work as usual. I took off early to pick up Steve from school, and we bought two new mountain bikes. If bicycling was OK for me, then we were going to enjoy it to the hilt. And we did, racing down Sycamore Canyon to the beach and back two or three times a week.

So my new disease introduced me to a delightful new sport, mountain biking. Marfan's syndrome proved a blessing in many ways. For one thing, it humbled me. I had always been proud of my healthy body. Based on a comprehensive examination back in 1979, a team of doctors told me I had the life expectancy of an 8-year-old (please note, not necessarily the mental age of an 8-year-old). Now I learned that I had the life expectancy of a nursing-home patient. My tall, slender frame was nothing but a body of death. A humbling thought indeed.

Marfan's also was a blessing in my marriage. After 15 years with Darlene I had begun taking her for granted. She was always there, you know, always the same. She was taking me for granted as well, so both of us were somewhat bored in our relationship. We loved each other and shared a total commitment, but we needed a fresh spark. In search of that we had attended a Marriage Encounter weekend, but I soon forgot to keep up with the things a good husband is supposed to be doing all the time—writing love notes and so on. Now the thought of my possible death jolted us out of our rut and thrust new life into our relationship. This past year of marriage has been the best by far, mainly because of my disease.

Marfan's syndrome also boosted my anticipation for God's great eternity. As a relatively young man, I had pictured myself fighting the battles of the Lord until Jesus comes. Now it looked as though I might lay down the sword early. Much as I enjoy my ministry, this was actually an exciting thought—certainly not business as usual, that's for sure.

It was also thrilling to realize that my faith could stand up to the threat of death. I can testify by experience that the gospel you have read in these pages really has the power to keep our hearts and minds in Christ Jesus, come what may. Unworthy though we are, through the blood of Christ we need not cower in the hour of judgment.

Another way Marfan's syndrome brought blessing involved my ability to relate to terminally ill people. I have a dear friend suffering from muscular dystrophy who appears doomed to an early grave. We've prayed many times, but the Lord seems to be letting him die. For years I doled out consolation texts, feeling somewhat like an outsider unworthy to help him with a problem I hadn't experienced. Now with a terminal illness myself, I could speak from my own pain and reach him on his level. He remarked during one of my visits, "I always appreciated what you had to say, but now that I know it comes from your own experience it means that much more."

I've watched a lot of godly people waste away from disease despite their magnificent faith. I've learned that true faith doesn't demand instant healing. Faith accepts healing in God's own time and way—whether immediately, or gradually, or at the resurrection when Jesus comes. You see, faith trusts God's timing to heal as well as His power to heal—whatever He knows is best for our lives and our service for Him. He never leads us differently than what we would choose for ourselves if we could see the end from the beginning, as He does, and understand His glorious purpose for our lives.

I had no question that God was leading in my life by allowing me to suffer with Marfan's. One of the greatest blessings He brought me was new friends—like Michael and Tara Flynn, a middle-aged couple I met at the National Marfan's Conference. Michael, who has Marfan's, has a remarkable testimony. In his tumultuous teenage years he got involved in narcotics—they helped him cope with his fears and insecurities. He also craved the popularity and excitement of being involved in the drug scene. Upon graduation from high school he became entangled in New Age teachings. The emphasis on positive thinking and good health helped him make the best of his Marfan's situation, and the philosophies of Eastern religion taught him patience in suffering. He also met quite a few friends through New Age fellowship. Michael became so deeply involved that a New Age center in Hawaii ordained him as a priest.

But then the ugly side of the New Age surfaced. Michael in his daily channeling realized that he was communicating with evil spirits—devils determined to destroy him. That became frightening. God in His mercy reached him with the good news of salvation through Christ. He became a Seventh-day Adventist along with his wife, Tara, a former Buddhist. Together they have a dynamic witness for Christ on the Hawaiian island of Kauai.

I spent one of the happiest weeks of my life visiting in their little apartment across from the beach, learning from Michael how to cope with Marfan's. Tara, a chiropractor, taught me special exercises to keep my back from succumbing to scoliosis.

Michael almost lost his life to Marfan's. His aorta had ballooned to the bursting point, and only an emergency operation at Loma Linda University Medical Center saved him. Dr. Carlos Schmidt, renowned as one of America's premier aortic surgeons, helped him just in time.

Michael isn't out of the woods yet, by any means. Other surgeries of high risk are needed to keep him alive. Through it all, he and Tara enjoy an amazing relationship in Christ. Rather than becoming obsessed with their problems, they are involved in a continual round of soul winning throughout Kauai. They are even planning an outreach for disadvantaged young people.

Michael and Tara Flynn are two of the most remarkable people I've met—and I wouldn't have known them had it not been for Marfan's syndrome. I've enjoyed all kinds of great relationships not otherwise possible. For example, in January of 1990 I attended the National Religious Broadcasters' convention in Washington, D.C. There I met Joni Eareckson Tada, the beloved quadriplegic who, from her wheelchair, operates the "Joni and Friends" ministry. We had a wonderful time discussing our handicaps and praising the Lord.

The day after we talked, both of us had hospital checkups scheduled. I took the train to Baltimore for my semiannual examination at Johns Hopkins Medical Center. The doctors hooked me up to the echocardiogram and ran their tests. Then they took a long time analyzing the results. I wondered what the problem was. Had the time come for open-heart surgery?

I sat waiting on the examination table, swinging my legs in anticipation of whatever new development might come along. At last the chief doctor stepped inside, shut the door, and probed me thoroughly with his stethoscope—saying hardly a word. Then he sat down and unleashed the shocking announcement.

"We've studied your echocardiogram very carefully. You don't have Marfan's syndrome."

"What!"

"That's right. Your heart shows no trace of deformity—no mitral valve prolapse. In fact, you have one of the healthiest hearts I've ever studied."

"But what about my long arms and all that?"

"You're just a tall person with a disproportionately large bone structure. But you don't have Marfan's syndrome."

"You mean I'm not going to die from an exploding aorta? You're sure of it?"

"No question about it. You're all clear."

"I can play basketball with my son again! I can dig up the garden. I can run and climb mountains and . . ."

"That's right. Go live your life to the full. Congratulations!" With that he stood up and shook my hand.

Can you believe it? After six months of living in the shadow of death, the Lord put me back in green pastures. I'm a normal person again.

What happened—was I healed? Or had the doctors misread my two previous echocardiograms?

I don't know. One of the cardiologists who examined me never felt convinced I had Marfan's, although the team of experts at Cedars-Sinai were unanimous in their diagnosis. I'll always remember that sad afternoon when they took my family into the office and told us I might die.

This much I do know. My first two echocardiograms showed MVP, but the past two have not. I also know that friends of mine across the country were praying. A little church in Massachusetts has a prayer service every morning at 5:00, and for months those dear saints begged God to heal me. You could never convince them that He hasn't done just that.

I have no burden to persuade anybody that God worked a miracle of healing for me. He certainly worked a miracle in other ways. He used a weird disease to bless beyond measure my relationship with Him, my marriage, and my ministry. On top of that, I've now got a healthy heart to serve Him for as long as He gives me strength.

"You turned my wailing into dancing; you removed my sackcloth and clothed me with joy, that my heart may sing to you and not be silent. O Lord my God, I will give you thanks forever" (Psalm 30:11, 12, NIV).

Free at Last

—————— 16 ——————

DARLENE AND I enjoy a wonderful life together with our children in Newbury Park, California. She works at the Adventist Media Center as a secretary. As for Steve and Christi, just entering their teenage years, any dad would be proud of them. Steve is terrific in sports, and Christi has real artistic talents.

Family togetherness means a lot to us. My travels take me away from home about a fourth of the time, but when I'm home we make the most of it. Every week I take one of the kids down to the beach. We have a great time roasting vegetarian burgers over an open fire, chasing the waves, and just talking. One night a week Darlene and I go out window-shopping, or maybe we visit someone. If we can't afford to eat at our favorite vegetarian restaurant, we might enjoy some frozen yogurt.

The best time for us as a family is on Sabbaths when I'm home. Friday at noon I pick up Steve and Christi from school and we stop at the supermarket for our "Sabbath goodies." That means our weekly ice cream, sugarless soda, and, best of all, chocolate chips for cookies that Darlene bakes. (Don't worry. My chocolate chips are only *semi*-sweet!) We wash the cars and vacuum the house, and hopefully by the time the sun sets, the preparation work is done. At sundown we gather around for worship. Darlene might read a story. We don't usually sing, since the kids don't enjoy that much, and we don't force them. Following sundown prayer it's time to bring out the Sabbath goodies.

Then, to round out Friday evening activities, we hop in the car and head for the Thousand Oaks Adventist Church for the TGIF (Thank God It's Friday) program. The service is youth-oriented, with lots of happy music, which I like as much as Steve and Christi do. Sometimes we stay home and play a Christian movie on our VCR.

On the Sabbath day itself, following church, we get together with friends for lunch, often with visitors from church. Then we go for a hike up nearby Mount Boney. My son and I might take our bicycles on a mountain trail. Sometimes we walk through Sycamore Canyon to an ocean lookout that doesn't feature the unspiritual distractions most beaches have on sunny weekend afternoons. Sabbath sundown comes all too soon, and it's back to another week of work. I miss my family when I travel. Sometimes I can take them with me, but usually it's not possible.

Everywhere I go I meet people who are afflicted with the same type of legalism by faith that I struggled with. As I try to help them find freedom in Jesus, some of them accuse me of lowering the standards of the church and being soft on sin.

This frustrates me because I continually emphasize the importance of no-nonsense obedience. All I'm asking is this: Let's not confuse the possibilities of Christian living with the requirement for salvation. The requirement for salvation is to accept by faith what Jesus offers us in exchange for what the world offers. Our lives will, of course, be drawn into harmony with God's law. Yet despite this miracle of new birth, we still fall short of Christ's glorious perfection.

To our shame, we even fall short of much of what we can attain in Christ. Does that mean we aren't saved?

Think about it. It might be possible for me to win 100 souls to Christ during the next 12 months. But suppose I don't—does that mean I'm lost? It might be possible for me to memorize the entire New Testament—but am I lost if instead I only read it and obey it? It's possible for me to be such a good father and husband that I run circles around Bill Cosby. But if I fail, am I a bad father and a failure as a Christian?

Always remember: Let's not confuse the requirement of salvation—a surrendered, trusting heart—with our potential for overcoming sin. If we compete with what Christ has already accomplished for us, we undermine our assurance of salvation. Victory over sin, something God intends to be an exciting adventure, becomes the heaviest of burdens and the gravest of all threats.

When I was a child I attended church school in Waldwick,

New Jersey. My brothers and I commuted on the Erie-Lackawanna train. Waiting at the station could get boring, so we would amuse ourselves by running on the rails to see how fast and how far we could go before we fell off the track.

It was fun, since there was no threat when we failed. When we fell, we simply picked ourselves up and tried again. But suppose we were running on the rails of a railroad trestle, high up there, when falling off would plunge us to our doom on the rocks below? The threat of losing our lives would turn something enjoyable into a terribly stressful experience. Do you see what the devil has done to spoil the glorious experience of victory in Jesus—making us feel lost when we fail?

True, many people abuse the freedom of forgiveness. Let them do it—they are only fooling themselves, indulging in their own damnation. Sincere Christians don't become lax in their obedience. The freedom of the gospel inspires them to walk faithfully and happily with Jesus.

With words such as these I try to help the burdened souls I meet at camp meetings. If they keep scolding me I'll ask them, "So you feel we need to qualify ourselves for heaven by attaining perfection? Very well, then, where were you back in 1973 when I fasted during Thanksgiving dinner? And where were you when I climbed that lonely mountain on those freezing nights?

"You try to teach me about perfection, but listen, I've been to hell and back, and believe me, trusting in the blood of Jesus Christ is our *only* hope of salvation."

Some people imagine that they can save the church by their suffocating scruples. Our church does have a massive problem with worldliness, but the solution is not for us to become modern-day Pharisees. Those who murdered their Messiah, you know, imagined themselves upholding the firm foundation of their religious standards. Is it possible that some of the strictest Sabbatarians of our day would have done the same thing to Jesus?

Without question, many zealous Adventists are in a backslidden condition, having fallen from their first love—fallen from grace. May God have mercy on them and help them repent. Their only hope of heaven is to humble themselves at the foot of the cross and cry, "Jesus, Son of David, have mercy on me!"

I've told my wife that if I die before she does, I want these words engraved on my tombstone: "Jesus, Son of David, have mercy on me!" No matter what we accomplish by God's grace, we never outgrow our need for His tender mercy.

A New Song for You Too

I waited patiently for the Lord;
    he turned to me and heard my cry.
He lifted me out of the slimy pit,
    out of the mud and mire;
he set my feet on a rock
    and gave me a firm place to stand.
He put a new song in my mouth,
    a hymn of praise to our God (Ps. 40:1-3, NIV).

A new song—that's what the Lord has given me. It's a much sweeter melody than I used to know. After reading these pages, you understand what I'm talking about.

In fact, you know a lot more about me than I wish you did—except for my hope that you've been helped. Perhaps now you don't feel so lonely, knowing that I've suffered some of the same spiritual pain you might be enduring.

I don't want to sound simplistic, but I firmly believe it's true: The gospel of Jesus Christ provides the solution to every personality hangup and emotional struggle you may have. That's not to say you don't need professional counseling—a licensed Christian counselor is equipped to apply skillfully the healing principles of God's grace to anyone's unique situation.

Of course, all the counseling in the world won't save your soul without faith in Jesus. It's my deep desire that you will enjoy the same fulfillment in Christ that I do. In case you somehow missed the simplicity of the gospel in the pages of this book, let me summarize it as clearly as I can.

What does it mean to have new life in Christ? And just as important, What doesn't it mean?

Our first step is when we come to recognize ourselves as lost sinners, unable to help ourselves. Like when you were a child vacationing with your family at Yosemite National Park.

You happily wandered along through the redwood forest when suddenly it dawned on you that you were lost. *No problem*, you thought, *I'll find my way back.* But each trail led off in the same direction—nowhere.

Then it started getting dark. Strange and scary noises made your heart flutter. Hungry grizzly bears lurked behind every tree. Finally, as you screamed in panic, you felt the strong arms of a park ranger pick you up and bundle you into his Jeep. In a moment you were sobbing safely in your parents' arms.

This world is a big, dark forest, and you and I have lost our way. At first we feel sure we can make it on our own. Then we realize that the hour is getting late and that dangers worse than grizzlies threaten our souls. Helpless and scared, we cry out to God. Jesus comes along and offers to rescue us.

Actually, it was 2,000 years ago when Jesus came to Bethlehem on His mission to save us. He was born in a dirty old barn, but He lived a clean and pure life. Never once did He do anything wrong, yet He died on the cross as a criminal. That was our death, the punishment we deserve. Now things are switched around. We who are guilty before God can receive the reward Jesus earned for us, eternal life. "By grace you have been saved through faith, and that not of yourselves, it is the gift of God, not of works, lest anyone should boast" (Eph. 2:8, 9, NKJV).

Here's how faith works. We decide that what Jesus offers is a lot better than what we now have in this world. So we repent of our old ways, praying: "Lord, be merciful to me a sinner. I want to be all Yours, and I want Jesus to be all mine!"

Immediately God accepts us as His children—as truly His own as Jesus Himself is. Instantly we become citizens of heaven, "giving thanks to the Father who has qualified us to be partakers of the inheritance of the saints in the light." In Jesus "we have redemption through His blood, the forgiveness of sins" (Col. 1:12, 14, NKJV).

Forgiveness is wonderful. But how do we get that new heart the Bible speaks of? When we accept Jesus, God's Holy Spirit creates in us a new spiritual birth. It's something like the miracle of the Christ child implanted within the virgin Mary—we can't understand how we are born again, but the result of a new heart transplant is obvious. It's obvious in our new attitude, a new willingness to live for Jesus and to love those around us.

What winning the gold medal means to Olympic athletes, living for Jesus means to every true believer. He is Number One. And just as the disciples long ago followed Jesus around Palestine, we also obediently follow Christ's will.

Obviously, we must know God's will if we are going to obey it. That's where daily Bible study comes in. Frequently we fail in our attempts to follow what the Bible teaches about God's will, but we can learn from our mistakes and grow. And as we keep entrusting our lives to God day by day, He keeps counting us perfect in Christ.

Maybe you still have questions. I'd love to hear from you. Just write to me, Martin Weber, c/o It Is Written, Box 0, Thousand Oaks, California 91360.

Meanwhile, even before you get all your questions answered, I urge you to surrender your life to God if you have not yet done so. He'll accept you just as you are, right now, and count you perfect in Christ.